Editor-in-Chief and Founder:
  Lyndon H. LaRouche, Jr.
Editorial Board: Lyndon H. LaRouche, Jr., Helga
  Zepp-LaRouche, Robert Ingraham, Tony
  Papert, Gerald Rose, Dennis Small, Jeffrey
  Steinberg, William Wertz
Co-Editors: Robert Ingraham, Tony Papert
Managing Editor: Nancy Spannaus
Technology: Marsha Freeman
Books: Katherine Notley
Ebooks: Richard Burden
Graphics: Alan Yue
Photos: Stuart Lewis
Circulation Manager: Stanley Ezrol

INTELLIGENCE DIRECTORS
Counterintelligence: Jeffrey Steinberg, Michele
  Steinberg
Economics: John Hoefle, Marcia Merry Baker,
  Paul Gallagher
History: Anton Chaitkin
Ibero-America: Dennis Small
Russia and Eastern Europe: Rachel Douglas
United States: Debra Freeman

INTERNATIONAL BUREAUS
Bogotá: Miriam Redondo
Berlin: Rainer Apel
Copenhagen: Tom Gillesberg
Houston: Harley Schlanger
Lima: Sara Madueño
Melbourne: Robert Barwick
Mexico City: Gerardo Castilleja Chávez
New Delhi: Ramtanu Maitra
Paris: Christine Bierre
Stockholm: Ulf Sandmark
United Nations, N.Y.C.: Leni Rubinstein
Washington, D.C.: William Jones
Wiesbaden: Göran Haglund

ON THE WEB
e-mail: eirns@larouchepub.com
www.larouchepub.com
www.executiveintelligencereview.com
www.larouchepub.com/eiw
Webmaster: John Sigerson
Assistant Webmaster: George Hollis
Editor, Arabic-language edition: Hussein Askary

EIR (ISSN 0273-6314) is published weekly
(50 issues), by EIR News Service, Inc.,
P.O. Box 17390, Washington, D.C. 20041-0390.
(703) 777-9451 ext. 415

European Headquarters: E.I.R. GmbH, Postfach
Bahnstrasse 9a, D-65205, Wiesbaden, Germany
Tel: 49-611-73650
Homepage: http://www.eirna.com
e-mail: eirna@eirna.com
Director: Georg Neudecker

Montreal, Canada: 514-461-1557

Denmark: EIR - Danmark, Sankt Knuds Vej 11,
basement left, DK-1903 Frederiksberg, Denmark.
Tel.: +45 35 43 60 40, Fax: +45 35 43 87 57. e-mail:
eirdk@hotmail.com.

Mexico City: EIR, Sor Juana Inés de la Cruz 242-2
Col. Agricultura C.P. 11360
Delegación M. Hidalgo, México D.F.
Tel. (5525) 5318-2301
eirmexico@gmail.com

Canada Post Publication Sales Agreement
#40683579

Postmaster: Send all address changes to EIR, P.O.
Box 17390, Washington, D.C. 20041-0390.

Signed articles in EIR represent the views of the
authors, and not necessarily those of the Editorial
Board.

I0407959

New Opportunity

EIR Contents

www.larouchepub.com Volume 44, Number 6, February 10, 2017

Cover This Week

Russian President Putin and Japanese Prime Minister Abe, at a Tokyo press conference, December 2016.

I. The New Agreement Among Nations

Therefore Choose Life

by Tony Papert

Feb. 7—President Trump's Feb. 10-11 summit with Japanese Prime Minister Shinzo Abe, offers the United States the opportunity to join in with the great new Eurasian-centered system of cooperation of the 21st Century—which includes Japan, China, Russia, and the more than 70 other nations, with 4.4 billion total population, which have joined in China's "Belt and Road Initiative" (BRI) of worldwide development corridors. It is indicative that Abe has prepared a contingency package for this upcoming summit, of Japanese hi-tech investment in the United States to create hundreds of thousands of good jobs.

Japanese media report that Prime Minister Abe has prepared a plan which includes large-scale investment in high-speed rail in Texas and California, along with other infrastructural investment, as well as mutual cooperation towards advanced nuclear power and other breakthrough technologies.

Japan's development of this package for Washington, must be understood as a spinoff of the revolutionary agreements being made between Japan and Russia over recent months. The two countries have been negotiating a peace agreement; they have officially been at war with each other for over 70 years. But these "peace negotiations" are unique in form: they would never have been possible outside the context of the new, Eurasia-centered agreement among nations—of which most Americans are still completely unaware.

Putin's Russia and Japan have decided to overcome an intractable territorial dispute, by means of the two nations' coming to understand and trust each other through ever-closer massive economic cooperation, in their common interest. When Prime Minister Abe met President Putin in Vladivostok, on Russia's Pacific coast, last September, he proposed eight points of eco-

Russian President Vladimir Putin (left) and Japan Prime Minister Shinzo Abe, at a joint press conference during Putin's December 2016 visit to Japan.

nomic cooperation, which included major Japanese investment to help develop the Russian Far East (or eastern Siberia). When Putin returned the visit in December, the eight points were reaffirmed and elaborated between them. Additionally, they agreed to joint economic development of the territory disputed between them, the Kuril Islands. Final resolution of the sovereignty dispute will follow the deepened trust to result from this cooperation.

When President Putin proposed this uniquely 21st-century path of negotiations with Japan, he, of course, had in mind Chinese President Xi Jinping's 2013 launching of the Belt and Road Initiative, a revolutionary vision of infrastructural development corridors linking all of Eurasia, spreading out into the Middle East and Africa, and, via a Bering Strait tunnel, into both American continents as well. As we have reported, the Belt and Road Initiative is the outgrowth of policy-proposals which Lyndon and Helga LaRouche have continuously fought for since 1988.

As President Putin himself noted, his other reference-point for this new path of negotiations with Japan, was the "Treaty of Good-Neighborliness and Friendly Cooperation between the People's Republic of China and the Russian Federation," signed in 2001 after thirty years of negotiations—negotiations which are still continuing today in a closer and deeper way, with ever more trust between the two sides. That 2001 treaty was a prerequisite for the BRI, while the negotiations for that treaty directly gave birth to the Shanghai Cooperation Organization, another important element of the new world constellation which is now open for the United States to join it.

The nations of Eurasia, led by Russia, China, and now Japan, are saying to the United States, "We've opened up a new way to live. Will you accept it and join it?" President Trump will not be a problem here, Lyndon LaRouche told associates on Feb. 6. Rather, U.S. adherence to the new agreement among the nations will be the way in which the new President can fulfill his campaign promise that no American who wants to work will be unable to find a job.

We have only a short period in which to consolidate this, LaRouche said. We have a solid group of leaders who firmly agree on principles of action; they must be consolidated as a unity. We've got a clean job, and it must remain that. What could ruin it, is if some third

EIRNS/Stuart Lewis

U.S. Capitol

party were allowed to barge in and try to impose its own, different principles.

The required principles are those of LaRouche's "Four New Laws." The initial leading forces have selected themselves. Others who want to enter must qualify themselves; they can't be allowed to just walk on in. We have to make that decision.

By this point, one can hear the hard-boiled reader asking, "But what are the chances of this?" That question reflects erroneous teachings about so-called probability against which Albert Einstein fought unceasingly over decades until his death in 1955. Statisticians are failed mathematicians, just as mathematicians are failed human beings. The fallacy of their notions of probability is especially obvious when they are applied to human affairs, as here.

Imagine that as you are crossing the street, a speeding vehicle jumps through a red light and heads directly at you, threatening to run you down. Our friend the statistician would lean into your ear and ask, "What are the odds that you can survive this?"

The Real Leaders of Congress Come Forward for Glass-Steagall

by Robert D. Ingraham

Feb. 5—On February 1, 2017, four leading members of the U.S. House of Representatives—Marcy Kaptur, Walter Jones, Tulsi Gabbard, and Tim Ryan—held a Press Conference, at which they announced the introduction into the new Congress of legislation, with twenty-six co-sponsors, to effect the immediate re-enactment of Franklin Roosevelt's original Glass-Steagall legislation. At that press conference these four Representatives both motivated the legislation and explained what has brought each of them to take a leading role in this effort. They described, in some detail, the destruction and suffering that has resulted from the Repeal of Glass-Steagall in 1999. At the same time they were explicit in their warnings, that a failure to re-institute Glass-Steagall, at this time, is threatening to plunge the United States into an even greater financial and economic crisis. (See the transcript of the press conference below.)

These four Representatives—three Democrats and one Republican—were explicit that they stand ready to work with President Trump if he honors his campaign pledge to restore Glass-Steagall. In a very real sense, although not stated in words, these four leaders, by their example, were calling on all members of Congress, both Democrats and Republicans, to "reach out across the aisle" and join in the urgent business of saving the nation from financial ruin.

The intensity of the mobilization to restore Glass-Steagall was underscored by several events which took place in the Capital in tandem with the press conference. On the same day as the four Representatives were speaking, President Trump's Press Secretary, Sean Spicer, in response to a question from *EIR* correspondent William Jones at the White House Press Conference, stated explicitly that President Trump remained committed to his campaign pledge to restore Glass-Steagall.

At the same time, three separate lobbying teams arrived in Washington, D.C. for a day-long effort of political discussions and lobbying. This included: a team of sixteen people from Ohio, Kentucky, and West Virginia, organized by "Our Revolution," which is circulating a petition in support of Glass-Steagall; a delegation of eighteen people from New York, New Jersey, and Pennsylvania, organized by LaRouche PAC; and a second LaRouche PAC team of six people

LaRouchePAC

Congresspersons Walter Jones, Tim Ryan, Tulsi Gabbard, and Marcy Kaptur

from Virginia and Maryland.

During the course of the day, these activists held meetings with twenty-five Congressional offices, in both the House and Senate. The effects of the partisan warfare being inflamed by George Soros and the establishment news media were on display in many of these meetings. Nevertheless, serious discussions occurred, often going well beyond the allotted time. The urgent necessity for Glass-Steagall to avert a new financial crash was recognized by many. Additionally, many of the deliberations were characterized by a more in-depth quality, focusing on elements of LaRouche's Four Laws, including the funding of a Hamiltonian National Bank for Infrastructure and Manufacturing, via swapping existing U.S. Treasury debt and the need for U.S.-Chinese-Russian collaboration on space exploration and development. All of this was posed from the standpoint of patriotic interest and the only pathway out of the current crisis.

Standing for the Nation's and the People's Interests

At a celebration of his 90th birthday, in 2012, Lyndon LaRouche forecast the end of the two-party system in America, stating that we had now reached a time of transition in which critical economic and national security concerns would begin to override the restrictions of partisan party politics.

Much as in 1856 when patriotic elements of the failed Democratic and Whig parties came together to give birth to what would become, five years later, the Lincoln Presidency, or the rallying of crucial elements of the Republican Party, in 1933, to give support to key initiatives of the new Franklin Roosevelt administration, American citizens—and their elected Representatives—now find themselves at a moment when the continued persistence of partisan "party politics" threatens to destroy any potential for the positive change which was created by the victory of Donald Trump in the November election over the Hillary Clinton/Barack Obama clique.

There are some individuals who now fear that, given the enraged intentions and efforts of Obama, Soros, and Wall Street, the Trump Administration may not be able to carry out its plans. The answer to such fears—the method whereby pessimism might be defeated—was delivered by Representatives Kaptur, Jones, Gabbard, and Ryan at their Feb. 1 press conference. That press conference marked a total break from the deluge of corrosive hyper-partisanship being led by ousted murderer Barack Obama himself, and fueled with millions of dollars of George Soros' drug-money. Here, instead, were patriots seeking to unite the House of Representatives, and unite it with the Senate and the Presidency, in behalf of a critical immediate step of vital national interest, and, in fact, of vital world interest.

What was personified, at that press conference, was the transcending of traditional party politics, just as LaRouche announced in 2012—to be replaced by a patriotic motivation. This necessary transformation of the political process is the absolutely necessary change which must occur if the nation is to go beyond the initial victory of Glass-Steagall re-enactment—toward a full embrace of LaRouche's "Four Laws" of June, 2014. Those Four Laws are an indissoluble unity. They are the principle without which nothing will work; this nation can only be saved by men and women of principle—and this is the principle. "This is what's real," as LaRouche stated on Feb. 3. "The rest is chatter."

Rep. Marcy Kaptur Reintroduces Glass-Steagall 'Return to Prudent Banking Act' H.R.790

Feb. 1—Here are the opening remarks by the four originating sponsors at their press conference, to re-introduce the Return to Prudent Banking Act, H.R.790, into the 115th Congress: Marcy Kaptur (D-Ohio), who introduced it into the 114th Congress; Tim Ryan (D-Ohio), Tulsi Gabbard (D-Hawaii), and Walter Jones (R-N.C.). The full press conference is posted to https://larouchepac.com/20170201/glass-steagall-bill-reintroduced-115th-congress-hr-790

Rep. Marcy Kaptur: I'm going to have my dear colleagues—Congressman Walter Jones of North Carolina, to join me up here at the podium, and also Congresswoman Tulsi Gabbard of Hawai'i, and Congressman Tim Ryan of Ohio. I thank them very, very much for joining us here today, and we want to welcome all of you,

Kaptur: We gather today on our country's behalf and for many, many citizens who didn't have the wherewithal to be here this morning, but nonetheless who would benefit by our common efforts.

This year marks the ninth anniversary of the greatest financial crisis in a generation. We're all old enough and our memories are good enough to remember that. That economic disaster nearly caused the destruction of our country's *entire* financial infrastructure and led to what history now calls "The Great Recession."

During the last nine years, if we look back and remember, Wall Street banks have succeeded and actually have made a great deal of money. Meanwhile, many, many Americans have continued—literally millions—to experience what we would term "financial failure." JPMorgan Chase, Bank of America, Citigroup, Wells Fargo, Goldman Sachs, and Morgan Stanley have all reported record profits during the recession *and* the years following. Wall Street in the last nine years has regained *all* its pre-crisis wealth *with interest,* while Main Street has yet to see a real recovery in so many communities from coast to coast.

And just to give you a couple of numbers: Fifteen years ago, the assets of the country's six largest banks were approximately seventeen percent of our total production, Gross Domestic Product—seventeen percent. Today, these top six banks hold $10.1 trillion in assets, *over half of our GDP*. This is too much power in too few hands. So not only have they profited handsomely, but they have come to command the major control centers of our economy.

Due to the financial crisis, JPMorgan Chase holds approximately 208,000 mortgages considered seriously delinquent, just in Ohio, while an excess of 700,000 homes are under water in our state. And Congressman Ryan and I know that problem well, and I know it's repeated in Hawai'i and repeated in North Carolina, as well.

During the 1990s, Wall Street's biggest banks and speculation houses concocted a fraudulent and greedy scheme to create false money. Then in 2008 their crime exploded. And you remember the collateralized debt obligations, the securitization of loans nearly destroyed capitalism itself. Their recklessness was so extreme it wiped out the net worth of *forty-four percent of His-panic-American households*—think about that—since the founding of the Republic; thirty-three percent of African-American households; and eleven percent of Caucasian households, respectively.

Being from Ohio, I can say in the Cleveland area, every area of Ohio—Toledo, Columbus, it doesn't matter where you go—Ohio was hit very, very hard. Actually harder than other parts of the country which were terribly harmed because of the nature of our manufacturing base and the type of state that we are.

So this taking by Wall Street was of historic dimension, never reimbursed to this day. It sucked out the wealth from *millions* of American families, and of course the movie, "Capitalism: A Love Story," documented that in real time, going back to 2008 and the days thereafter. https://www.youtube.com/watch?v=CkTkYQkG13w

It is time for Congress that these failures in our banking system are never repeated, and that is why we are here today. And I thank my colleagues so very, very much for joining me, to build on the momentum and a movement to reinstate Glass-Steagall, to *separate* prudent commercial banking from speculation.

Since last summer, 15 state legislatures have introduced resolutions calling for Congress to reinstate Glass-Steagall, and Democrats and Republicans have memorialized support for Glass-Steagall in their respective political platforms, which was an enormous achievement by all of you, and others around our country who have worked for this for a very long time, who have long memories.

Even President Trump has declared his support for a new Glass-Steagall law, and we are obligated to work with him to create that. So I was proud to join the 57 members of the House who several years ago voted against the Gramm-Leach-Bliley Act which overturned the Glass-Steagall Act. And after I was one of those that voted against it, I remember that vote well in the late 1990s; it released a greed and abandon on Wall Street that had been capped since the Great Depression years of the early 20th century. The law was a clear signal, by removing it, that Wall Street was in charge. And speculation houses grew larger and riskier, and, as we predicted, the house came crashing down. And American taxpayers were given the bill, when the deregulated financial sector fell apart.

I'm not sure we still know the whole truth. History will track and help to right the reality of all of that. But we know that Wall Street has sunk its teeth deeply into the flesh of our Republic, influencing more and more who is elevated to office, but also how money flows, how money flows in this economy. I'm amazed when I go to audiences in my district and I say, "How many of you are paying a mortgage to one of the six institutions I just mentioned? How many of you have your student loan or your car loan end up in their hands? You ask at your church, you ask at your school, you ask in your neighborhood meetings, you ask in your veterans posts, you will find those names: They control the levers of this economy." And you've noticed, even with the new administration, where the appointees who are being selected worked before they came to the new administration: We have at least seven from Goldman Sachs alone.

These banks have to be made prudent again, and restoring Glass-Steagall is a first step, among many other items that this Congress must address, like campaign finance reform, to drain the swamp, really; better trade deals, and better deals for American workers.

I would now like to call upon my dear colleague from the state of North Carolina, who has been an original cosponsor and leader on this for many, many years: Walter Jones, one of the most honorable and thoughtful, and really, a man of great conscience for our House

President Franklin Roosevelt signs the original Glass-Steagall Act.

that members on both sides of the aisle so deeply respect. Walter, thank you for being with us today. [applause]

Rep. Walter Jones: Marcy, thank you very much. And I cannot add much to what she told you about the history and the threat to our nation. And so I'm going to make a few comments, and I first will tell you that I've said many times in my district, the two worst votes I cast as a Member of Congress: First was the Iraq War, that was a very unnecessary war; and the second was Repealing Glass-Steagall. So, since that time, I came out in 2003 or 2004 with Ron Paul, Neil Abercrombie, and Dennis Kucinich to set up a timetable to get out of Iraq. So, I'm trying to make amends for that sin.

The second sin, which I've already mentioned was the repeal of Glass-Steagall. So, after seeing what has happened with the financial markets, it became pretty evident that I had made a bad mistake, no question about it. So, my dear friend, Marcy Kaptur, who's taken the lead on this issue for a number of years, and I, had many conversations on the floor of the House and she knew of my admitting publicly that I had made a mistake; and she knew and I knew that she was going to try to correct this problem of trying to have a reinstatement of a Glass-Steagall. And so she and I have worked together. She's been the lead, I've been the half-back. She's been the quarter-back and the coach, but I am

there as a half-back and I can either run with the ball or I can block.

I am pleased that she made reference to Donald Trump and I'll read one paragraph and then I'm going to close. "United States Republican Presidential candidate Donald Trump on Wednesday called for a '21st-century version of the 1933 Glass-Steagall law that required the separation of commercial and investment banking, a change the Republican Party also supported in the 2016 Policy Platform." [Reuters, Oct.26]

I intend to be very proactive. As soon as the White House gets a little bit better organized, I intend to reach out to his advisors on commercial matters and remind them of the position that he and my party have taken on a reinstatement of this Glass-Steagall Act.

So with that, Marcy, I want you to know that I am committed to this, as much as anything I've ever been committed to. Again, I am your half-back. I think Tim is the defensive end [laughter]—but I am your half-back and I will be out there and take every step in whatever you need to do.

But as she has said, and this is my close, "You are the key to this." The American people have got to understand the attack and the damage that has been *done to them* by the fact that we repealed Glass-Steagall. Let's make this a *victory*, this year of 2017. Thank you. [applause]

Rep. Kaptur: Thank you, Walter. Thank you so very, very much. I'm going to call on Tulsi Gabbard now. She has another committee hearing that she has to go to—just an electric, talented Congresswoman from the state of Hawai'i.

Rep. Tulsi Gabbard: Thank you. Good morning and aloha. It's great to start our day here with you, dealing with and addressing this incredibly important issue. I want to thank Marcy and Walter for your leadership on this, persisting through many great challenges to continue to bring the plight of the American people to the forefront. When we're dealing in the highly divisive, partisan environment that we have, what I hear from folks in my district in Hawai'i and from people across the country is a demand that leaders in Washington hear their voices, to understand the challenges that they and their families are facing, the struggles that they continue to go through because of situations like this, because of the repeal of Glass-Steagall; because of what the Wall Street banks have done to them. I couldn't be more proud to be cosponsor of this legislation, because it seeks to address a wrong, again, that people are still suffering the consequences of.

We have continued to see the rise of these banks that were too-big-to-fail back then, that are even bigger, now. We continue to see the consequences of the repeal of Glass-Steagall first-hand in communities like mine and in communities across the country, where Wall Street banks have been allowed to conduct their risky investment practices with the American people's money. They have been allowed to continue to gamble for their bottom line and their profit on the backs of the American people. This is unacceptable.

This is not a partisan issue. This is an issue that is important to the American people, and why you see bipartisan support for this important legislation. I've long been a proponent of restoring the Glass-Steagall Act and look forward to being able to continue to work with allies and partners here in Congress, in the White House, and most importantly, the American people, whose voices must be heard. Thank you so much. [applause]

Rep. Kaptur: Thank you Tulsi, and thank you for your work on the Democratic Platform, in order to get this issue inserted, this past year. That has helped us so very, very much; thank you.

I'd now like to call on someone whose district and whose state has lived this problem for many, many years now—our very able and energetic and brilliant Congressman from Youngstown, Ohio, Tim Ryan.

Rep. Tim Ryan: Thank you. I want to thank Marcy and Walter, too and just let Walter know that as a Cleveland Browns fan, you don't want me participating in any blocking or tackling, or throwing or running. I'll sit this out, and help from the sidelines, maybe.

I want to thank Marcy and Walter for doing this, and sticking to this. Walter mentioned the word "sin," and I think this repeal was the original sin of the downward spiral of our economy that led to completely wiping out neighborhoods in my Congressional District and all across the state and country. And so this act is a way for us to, as us Catholics would say, "go to confession," and have this stain removed from the body politic in the United States, and hopefully start to restore some level of sanity to our banking system. And this is a great first step.

And we've seen the heartache, we've seen the neighborhoods wiped out, the tax base eroded in so many communities, the school districts that were affected by so much of this, and just a lot of heartache down the line. And so, let's get back to a place where we're actually operating from a principled place that puts the people before the banks. And this is a great opportunity, I think; as Walter said, the President of the United States has made this a priority. There are plenty of Democrats who want to continue to make this a priority, and I think even more so if they think it's possible. So this is a great first step. I'm happy to be a part of this and continue to support this, and continue to support my colleagues and try to rectify some of these problems that devastated our state, and which—and Marcy knows this—we're still recovering from. We're still not anywhere close to being out of the woods. And hopefully once we plug this hole, we can really begin the process of really rebuilding and giving the American people the kind of government they really deserve. Thank you.

Rep. Kaptur: Thank you, Tim, so very, very much. I'm old enough to remember when there were savings and loan institutions in our country, and literally, you could earn 9% interest. And, then there were crises in the 1980s in California, housing crises, and legislation came before Congress to get rid of the savings and loan institutions which had been especially set up to make mortgages and to handle the real estate market. I voted against the changes that gave the commercial banks the power to absorb the savings and loan institutions, essentially.

And since that time, what we have seen happen, commercial loans have a seven-year life, a mortgage has a thirty or forty-year life; they're different species. But they mixed them together, and then what happened was Wall Street, during the 1990s, did exactly what we thought they would do: The commercial banks then tried to get into the mortgage business, but guess what they found out? They couldn't make as much money as they could with their commercial loan portfolio—as fast as they wanted to! And so that's when they invented the instruments like securitization, and collateralized debt obligations, to try to jimmy-rig the system, because it wasn't producing profits fast enough.

And by then, of course, they removed the laws that separated speculation from banking! Yeah, we have a stock market: If you want to invest and you lose your money in these highly risky instruments, you have a right to do that—but not to put in jeopardy the savings of the American people. And the largest form of the savings we have is the home mortgage.

So what we've seen is a revolution really in the banking system, happen slowly—it happened slowly, and people missed some of what happened here; legislatively that set the new ground rules for this greed and for this abandonment. So what we have is, we have a system now, where the housing market is floating in this very speculative world, and these very same institutions that are doing the high risk investments, are also receiving your mortgage payments. And it's a very combustible mix: We saw that in 2008. So this is what's going on. And every American citizen who has a savings account, which is a good thing to have a savings account to save for the future—it shows you're prudent, it shows you're managing your money well—show me any place in the country that's paying over two percent for savings! You're more likely [to get] 0.1 or 0.5, if you're lucky. I think the highest one in Toledo is 1.7, you know, in a credit union—and only one credit union is doing that, and I'm not sure they're Federally insured. I have to check that one out. [laughter]

But you know, you think about really robbing the American people, with the type of interest rates, and my brother says, "You know what, Marcy, you know what this is like? You have to pay the bank to take your money!" I say, "Yeah, what kind of system is this?!" And then, if you have a student loan, the interest going up each couple years, the rate for those students goes up. So really, the tables are turned the wrong way on the American people. And the banks need to pay a higher rate for renting your money. And that's what this is all about.

Four Powers To Bury the British System: From Franklin Roosevelt To Lyndon LaRouche

by J. Philip Rubinstein

Feb. 1—On October 10, 2009, Lyndon LaRouche delivered an address to the Seventh Annual Session of the World Public Forum Dialogue of Civilizations, on the Island of Rhodes in Greece,[1] wherein he stated:

> Therefore, the task, as I defined it, is, if Russia, and the United States, and China, and India, agree, as a group of countries to initiate and force a reorganization of the world financial and credit system, under these conditions, with long term agreements, of the same type that Franklin Roosevelt had uttered before his death, in 1944, under key nations, the intention of Roosevelt all these years later, could have been realized, and we could do that today.

What FDR, and LaRouche, foresaw as the way to replace the inhuman British System of world finance, would now be in effect were the United States to join Russia, India, and China with its One Belt One Road policy of Eurasian development—the latter, in fact, a part of LaRouche's World Land-Bridge. Presidents Putin and Xi have been especially committed to this and have offered an open invitation to the United States to join. Donald Trump has been brought to the Presidency of the United States not by a chaotic, populist impulse in the U.S. electorate, but by a global change brought on by the collapse of the London-Wall Street system, and the live potential of a new economic world as seen in China. This Four Power combination would effect the complete replacement of the two hundred-plus years of the British Empire.

That 2009 intention of what Lyndon LaRouche proposed was echoed by Russian Foreign Minister Sergei Lavrov in a speech delivered on January 25 of this year to the lower house of the Russian Legislature, the Duma:

> We believe that as Russia, the U.S. and China build their relations, this triangle should not be closed or directed toward some projects that could worry other states. [They should be] open and fair. I am convinced that the economic structure of Russia, the U.S. and China is such that there is a great deal of complementarity in the material and economic sphere.
>
> As for international security problems, these three countries play a very important role. Russia and China have restrained attempts to introduce confrontational, force-based solutions into world politics. We expect that Donald Trump, who has confirmed his commitment to focus primarily on US [domestic] problems and to abandon interference in the internal affairs of other states, will do the same...

The Chinese Foreign Ministry's spokesman, Hua Chunying, responded to Lavrov's statement, saying, according to Tass, "China, Russia and the U.S. are the leading global powers, and they are the permanent members of the UN Security Council. We have great responsibility for global peace, stability and development." Beijing has been deepening relations of strategic partnership and cooperation with Russia, and has also been making efforts to develop trust-based relations with the U.S., she said, "Therefore, China plans to intensify cooperation with the U.S. and Russia and to make common contribution to solving the tasks and challenges of the modern world."

She also noted that the Russian side has repeatedly said that it attaches great importance to Russian-Chinese relations and gives a high assessment to them. "We welcome this," she said, adding that the relations of

---

1. From *EIR*, October 23, 2009 http://www.larouchepub.com/lar/2009/3641lar_spch_rhodes.html

strategic partnership and cooperation between the two countries have reached the highest level, and both sides plan to jointly work on the issues of regional and global peace, stability and development.

The fourth of the "Four Powers" named by Lyndon LaRouche, and organized earlier by Franklin Delano Roosevelt in his own struggle to put an end to the world rule of the British Empire—is India. On January 26, India's Republic Day, Russian President Putin sent greetings to India's President and Prime Minister, which said that the special and privileged strategic partnership with India is an invariable priority in Russia's foreign policy.

What is it that, up until now, has kept the United States out of this Four Power arrangement of peace and economic cooperation? What opposition does President Trump now face were he to act as Lyndon and Helga LaRouche have proposed?

Consider: Why did FDR's death mean, that his vision, the vision of the man who led America out of the Great Depression and to victory in World War II, would fade until seventy years after his death? Why has Lyndon LaRouche been nearly alone in the fight for FDR's conception in the United States?

The following may help produce a basis for an insight into this, and how to change it now, with the opportunity provided by the recent Presidential election.

Carol M. Highsmith

Room Three of the Franklin Delano Roosevelt Memorial, Washington, D.C.

The Imperial 'Special Relationship'

The present Prime Minister of the United Kingdom, Theresa May, herself ironically raised to Prime Minister by the resignation of her predecessor in the wake of the British vote to leave the European Union, raced to be the first leader to meet President Trump. Her mission: to assure the continuation of the cherished "Special Relationship," coined, if not created, by Winston Churchill.

This behavior has numerous precedents in the interval from FDR to the present. The British know they cannot rule without the United States. This became crystal clear when their creation, Adolf Hitler, instead of going East and attacking Russia in 1940, as British elites intended, instead turned West as Hitler's military command knew they must. Britain's "Frankenstein's monster," Adolf Hitler, thus forced the British to ally with their original target, the USSR. This was a bitter lesson for the London oligarchy. As Churchill put it, "After this war, we will be weak. We will have no money and no strength, and we will lie between the two great powers of the USA and the USSR." (*Six Months in 1945* by Michael Dobbs, p.103). For the British Empire to survive, after 1945, this meant that Britain had to control the U.S. and pit America against the Soviets, which could not be done with Roosevelt alive.

This is the real theme of the last seventy years in different variations. Looking backward in time, we have Tony Blair, in Chicago in 1999, enunciating the Regime Change policy of "Right to Protect," and the end of Westphalian Sovereignty. This led to a policy of perpetual war under George W. Bush, a policy which intensified under Barack Obama. It was Blair who was the author of the lie that Iraq possessed weapons of mass destruction in the infamous "dodgy dossier." He claimed that Iraq could deliver a nuclear bomb on forty-five minutes notice, and he became the key confidant to Bush in the second Iraq war. The result was the death of hundreds of thousands of civilians and a disaster for the U.S. With these credentials Blair then became the chief proponent and mentor of Obama.

A bit further back we have Margaret Thatcher, famously "stiffening the resolve" of George H.W. Bush— clearly the Bush family had some limitations despite their loyalty to the Crown. This gave us the first Iraq war. A decade earlier, when Reagan evinced some reluctance to join the British in the Malvinas war, Thatcher turned to anglophile Secretary of Defense Caspar Weinberger to draw the U.S. in on the British side, violating the Monroe Doctrine.

This is not to say these efforts always succeeded. The British failed in the case of the Suez crisis of 1956, when Eisenhower refused to go along. The Prime Minister of the time, Anthony Eden, was forced to resign. Despite these singular exceptions, since Roosevelt's death, the UK-USA "Special Relationship" has been the core British necessity for maintaining the Empire.

Roosevelt Battles the Empire

This reality governed the relationship of FDR and Churchill through World War II. Churchill intended from the very beginning to direct the U.S. war effort. Within days of Pearl Harbor he arrived at the White House, to stay for over a month. His goal was to ensure some control over the U.S. military actions, but even more to guarantee the primacy of the alliance with Britain.

Franklin Roosevelt, however, had other ideas, as did General Marshall and others, both regarding military, as well as political questions. For Roosevelt, this was an alliance of necessity, but it was a difficult one, and it showed most clearly on the issue of the colonies, the special economic rules for them, as well as on the question of the Soviet Union. For FDR, World War II was to be a war of liberation from the very system that was destroying the world with depression and war. There was no point to fighting fascism only to continue the inhumanity of colonialism. As reported by Elliot Roosevelt and others, Churchill became furious at even the suggestion that India, the crown jewel of the Empire, might gain independence at the end of the war.

Through the course of the war, FDR, as well as Generals MacArthur and Eisenhower, realized that general war was no longer a means to settle political disputes among nations. The horror of modern warfare was too great, even before the arrival of nuclear weapons. Roosevelt envisioned a United Nations Organization (which was the name of the war-time alliance) as a place to debate and find solutions to conflict among sovereign nations freed from colonialism. FDR had a clear idea of the development needed to truly liberate colonies. His vast geographical knowledge was essentially a map of needed development projects, such as he envisioned when he flew over North Africa and proposed to an uninterested Saudi king Ibn Saud. The great Four Corners projects that he had led in the U.S. were the paradigm for what Roosevelt envisioned globally.

US Army

Stalin, Roosevelt and Churchill at the Tehran Conference, 1943

At the same time FDR saw the need for a core of leading nations to make this effective. Despite their differing war "objectives," the Big Three of World War II (America, the Soviet Union and Britain) were a military necessity. For the post-war period, this would become a Big Four. In fact, it was Roosevelt who insisted that China be part of a Big Four during the war, despite the opposition of both Stalin and Churchill. The future would require a solid foundation with the United States, the Soviet Union, leading developing and newly independent nations, and the nation called the United Kingdom.

FDR's conception was not a pipe-dream, as it is often portrayed today. Nor did he think he could manipulate Stalin by some personal tie. There was good reason for Stalin's belief that the West did not mind the USSR taking the brunt of the war, and a great deal of distrust had to be overcome. FDR also knew that Stalin and the Soviets were aware that they would need ten to twenty years to rebuild after the destruction of the war, and that they would need help from the West. Therefore by developing some common basis in securing peace and development, trust could be built, and a new global directionality might be realized.

China and India

China, at the same time, was an independent nation and represented the future of the underdeveloped world. FDR's confidante and global representative Harry Hopkins, in a report in August, 1945, stated,

> If I were to indicate a country in which the United States, for the next hundred years, had the greatest interest from political and economic points of view, I would name the Republic of China. With the defeat of Japan, China will become one the greatest land-powers on earth. I do not say that she will be one of the most powerful for many years to come, but she will have regained her heritage in Manchuria, and we hope there will arise out of the welter of war a unified China.

It is clear that this was Roosevelt's concept of the postwar era.

Churchill was appalled by all of this. He viewed India and China with typical racist arrogance. FDR had approved Chiang Kai-shek visiting Mahatma Gandhi in India to attempt to organize his support, at least logistically, against Japan. For Gandhi and India there was little to choose between the British Empire and the German-Japan axis. Churchill refused to allow Chiang to meet at Gandhi's home and interfere in India. Despite this, they did meet for five hours, after which Chiang received a letter from Gandhi, in which he wrote to Chiang, that "I consider the five hours of frank discussion that we had in Calcutta as the most satisfying and unforgettable experience in my life." Following this, Chiang sent a note to FDR on the need for Britain and Holland to copy the American example in the Philippines and unequivocally promise full independence to all their colonies. This, Chiang said, was the only way to ensure the true loyalty of colonial peoples to the allied cause. In his message he quoted at length from his conversation with "an Indian friend." FDR passed this on to Churchill, who was outraged, not just at the call for India to be independent, but the mere audacity of China and America to meddle in Imperial affairs (*The Generalissimo* by Jay Taylor). When FDR intimated a comparison of India with the U.S., he was told, "it is none of your business."

Two Incompatible Visions

The British held the same view at Bretton Woods. This was not simply some peculiarity of Churchill. At Bretton Woods, while preaching free trade, as usual, the entire British delegation rejected any discussion of trade preferences with their colonies.

As to the Soviet Union, British strategy was always to allow the Soviets to fight it out with Hitler, or minimally, to bear the brunt of the war. When Hitler turned west, the alliance with the USSR became necessary, but the destruction of the Soviet Union remained paramount policy. At the same time, everything was done to keep Roosevelt from succeeding in organizing a relationship with Stalin based on the need for economic development. To this day, the lie is repeated that FDR was weak at Yalta and deluded about his ability to influence Stalin. In truth, FDR was dying, but it was the British who were waiting for him to pass, to overturn his leadership. Roosevelt's strategy, throughout the entirety of the war, was clear, and he stuck to it. His distance from Churchill was due to a divide over the peace and the future. For Roosevelt it meant the end of the colonial world and the end of want, the key to the Four Freedoms.

Churchill was in fact preparing for the cold war, already referring to the "iron veil" well before his Fulton, Missouri speech, and prior to FDR's passing from the scene. Churchill insisted on blowing Yalta up over Poland, but the truth is, that he had proposed the boundaries already to Stalin, just as he had proposed the division of the Balkans on a piece of paper he handed to Stalin in a private meeting—so much for the hero of the neo-cons.

The role of the British in stalling the Western Front is well known. Less well known are its effects. It should be clear that FDR and Chief of Staff General Marshall saw the Western Front as the only way to win the war and alleviate the enormous pressure on the Red Army. The constant sabotage by the British, ironically, gave Stalin a stronger hand and even moral advantage, given that the Red army did by far most of the fighting to the end. Fully two thirds of the German soldiers killed during the war were in the East. Overall, eight million Russian soldiers were killed or missing versus 416,000 Americans and 383,000 British. Even more, total Soviet losses were twenty-seven million, including civilians. These losses were incomparable and staggering.

As the British intended, the divide between the Russian and American allies became much more intense with the death of FDR and the dropping of the A-bomb. Stalin was not told of the developments around the bomb until the very end. Truman, Churchill and others, like confederate Secretary of State James Byrnes, viewed the bomb as the great equalizer to the Soviet advantage on the ground—really more than equal.

Truman and Churchill were almost giddy when

news of the successful bomb test was received at Potsdam. The nuclear cold war was on, if not won, and the likes of Bertrand Russell were calling for nuclear bombing of the Soviet Union. Russell wanted nuclear superiority to enforce world government.

FDR's vision of a UNO secured by a Four Power agreement of America, Russia, China and Britain (France was viewed as a partner of the British) emphatically meant a developing relationship to a rebuilding of the Soviet Union, as well as of China, as a future force representative of the developing sector. He had expressed this in the Four Freedoms: from want, from fear, of speech, of belief. After 1945, all this was twisted into unrecognizable form, into a stratagem of more war and poverty. All that was to be left was the "Special Relationship" with the British Empire.

Despite figures like Eisenhower, MacArthur and JFK, this orientation increasingly took over, until it finally dominated U.S. policy making, down to the present day. By the Fall of the Berlin Wall in 1989 and the collapse of the Soviet Union in 1991, with the subsequent Bush and Obama administrations, it appeared that the takeover was complete. The Achilles Heel, however, was foreseen by LaRouche even as the Wall fell. The London-Wall Street Axis was rotten ripe itself. There has been an ongoing collapse of the trans-Atlantic British financial system of increasing intensity, especially since 2007-2008. The seventy year long "Special Relationship" is now at a dead end, and there is no way out.

A Return to Roosevelt's Vision

FDR's Four Powers, as exemplified in the policy of the World Land-Bridge, is the active policy of China, supported by Russia, in effect today. Other nations are increasingly taking part, led by the BRICS group, most especially India. This includes building new financial institutions like the Asian Infrastructure Investment Bank (AIIB) with up to seventy or more participants.

As can be seen in the quotes with which we began, Russia and China, under the leadership of Putin and Xi, are fully committed to this policy, and have offered an open hand to the troubled United States. Without the "Special Relationship," the British System is doomed to be replaced by a New Paradigm. The question that will determine the possibility of avoiding a catastrophe of war or chaos provoked by this dying Empire is—

Presidential candidate Lyndon LaRouche (left) conversing with Presidential candidate Ronald Reagan at a campaign event in New Hampshire in 1980.

Which way the United States?

During the American Presidential campaign, Donald Trump pledged to reinstate FDR's Glass-Steagall banking regulation, separating out speculative financial activity. This would open the door to the full LaRouche policy of Hamiltonian credit and crash scientific programs to increase the productivity of labor, making the U.S. a full partner in world progress. Lyndon LaRouche, as a young man serving in the India-Burma theater at the end of the war, pledged himself to fulfill FDR's mission, and with the backing of a knowledgeable American people it can be done now.

Allow yourself a few moments of unfettered imagination; imagine a world where the United States—the only nation to put men on the Moon and bring them back—reinvigorates its nearly destroyed space program, by joining with the active and highly successful Chinese program, with the Russian capabilities, with the India that successfully launched an orbiter to Mars in 2013, with the European space program, and others—in a Four Powers-led Extra-Terrestrial Policy for the future of humanity. Or, imagine a truly unified effort to tackle the breakthroughs needed to utilize fusion power and solve further problems in our knowledge of the micro-world. What can be done in advancing conceptions of biology using the mixture of science available globally?

How many high level jobs would be needed? How many highly developed youth with a breadth of education and character to create for the further future would be needed? What would we begin to know about each other? What would it mean for our knowledge of Mankind?

The Win-Win Solution: One Belt, One Road

This is an edited transcript of Helga Zepp-LaRouche's keynote address to the Schiller Institute conference in Manhattan on Feb. 4.

Dennis Speed: My name is Dennis Speed, and on behalf of the Schiller Institute, I want to welcome you to today's conference. This is part of a series of conferences that the Schiller Institute has been sponsoring for several years now, on a dialogue of cultures and civilization, but this conference has a very specific significance.

America and the new American Presidency can and should commit itself to a new economic outlook on behalf of all humanity. Today's conference is devoted to exploring the possibilities of radically transforming the relationship between China and the United States for the better, but that is merely one aspect of our purpose.

The World Land-Bridge proposal advocated by Helga Zepp-LaRouche and the Schiller Institute—first advocated over 20 years ago and now refined and updated—is not a proposal for mere infrastructure development, but for a whole new economic platform and a new outlook on humanity:

• The prospect for a joint space mission to the Moon combining India, China, Russia, Japan, the United States, and other countries;

• The joint crash development of advanced nuclear power systems and of thermonuclear fusion power generation;

• Joint collaboration to end starvation, drought, and disease in Africa by building the largest water, rail, and power projects in history.

Helga Zepp-LaRouche addressing the Feb. 4 Schiller Institute conference in New York City.

This is the human economy that we can now create.

To tell you how this future can be attained and how that new economic platform can create a new human culture that will allow humanity to achieve adulthood and rise above the infantile diseases of war and conflict, it is my pleasure to introduce our first speaker, the founder and head of the Schiller Institutes, Helga Zepp-LaRouche. [applause]

Helga Zepp-LaRouche: Ladies and gentlemen, I'm very happy to be able to address you even if it is only electronically, but I am happy to be with you, because this is very much a defining moment in history. The chances to build a completely new paradigm in the world is within reach and could be a reality in a very short period of time.

That may be difficult to believe if you look at the world as it is right now, which is clearly in the biggest uproar I have experienced, maybe in my lifetime. The election of President Trump in the United States has caused violent reactions in the United States and in Europe, and I have never seen a situation in which an American President, who just got democratically elected, was met with such a fierce opposition.

Therefore, I think it is important to situate this election in the broader context, because the election of President Trump was not the first such uproar. Really, the first one was last June: The Brexit vote of the British people, the decision to leave the EU, already caused a shock. Then you had the election of Trump, and then very shortly after that you had a referendum in Italy

President Donald Trump

White House

deciding on the change of the Constitution, where 60% of the Italians voted "no" against the policies of the EU. You have to see Brexit, the Trump vote, and the "No" vote in that referendum as a common development.

The Foreign Minister of Germany, Mr. Steinmeier, characterized the election of Trump as the end of the order of the 20th Century. Obviously, that is what is going on because you have, as the common denominator between all these revolutionary changes, the fact that the neo-liberal world order, at least of the 26 years after the collapse of the Soviet Union, indeed has ended and it will never come back.

You have even the more extreme reaction of Mr. Donald Tusk, who is the present President of the European Council, who just wrote a letter to the 27 remaining heads of state of the EU, in which he said that the Trump Administration represents the same threat to Europe as the newly "assertive China," an "aggressive" Russia, and "wars, terror, and anarchy in the Middle East and Africa."

Even if you discount the fact that Mr. Tusk is Polish and they sometimes have peculiar views these days— but to put Trump on the same level as ISIS? Well, it was very clear from Day One, that the representatives of the collapsed unipolar world did not accept Trump as a President. Already in the foreground of the election, you had the hand of MI6 very clearly in the fake dossier of MI6 agent Christopher Steele, which basically tried to argue that Trump won the election only because Putin hacked into the e-mails of the Democratic Party

and that therefore Putin stole the election from Hillary Clinton—a ridiculous view, which is still to the present day proclaimed by Hillary Clinton and by many of the Democrats.

The British Empire Against the U.S.

The characterization of these demonstrations against Trump as a "color revolution," was my first view on the matter, but President Putin also gave it the same name. If you look at what happened with the color revolutions, you had the same characteristics in the Orange Revolution in Ukraine in 2004 and the so-called Rose Revolution in Georgia. This was the same kind of process as in the Arab Spring, as in the attempted but failed White Revolution against Russia, and also in the Yellow Revolution with the yellow umbrellas in Hong Kong, which did not go very far. And the governments of both Russia and China characterized these efforts at color revolutions as a form of war. Putin basically called it "a Maidan" against Trump, and that is what it is: It is by the same people, by the same political apparatus, and for the same motives.

To understand what is going on, in my view, one has to consider the entire history of the United States, because the British Empire at the time of the American Revolution, never accepted that America, their most important colony, would become independent, and they tried to reverse that, first, in a military way, with the War of 1812. They tried the same thing with the Civil War, when the British Empire was allied with the Confederacy against Lincoln.

But after that, they realized it would not be possible to militarily reverse the independence of the United States. Therefore, they changed tactics, and from that point on said, "OK, if we can convince the American establishment to rule the world as an empire based on the British model, then we have it." And they succeeded to a very large extent in accomplishing that. This was the basis of the American policy since Teddy Roosevelt, with the very short interruptions of Franklin D. Roosevelt, and to a certain extent, John F. Kennedy.

With the collapse of the Soviet Union, the neo-cons saw their moment and that of the British to establish this principle of a unipolar world, where basically they would eliminate every government which would not submit to this unipolar world through color revolutions, through regime change, or through wars based on lies,

British troops burning the White House in the War of 1812.

as it was in the case in Afghanistan, Iraq, and Libya. They tried the same thing in Syria.

If you take the word or the concept of "globalization," as just being another word for this Anglo-American Empire—a system where the profit of the few is what counts, the system where the rich became *unbelievably* rich, where the poor became poorer, and the middle class was vanishing—well, this left a lot of people who felt left out, the so-called "deplorables," as Hillary Clinton called them.

People had this tremendous sense of injustice caused by the EU, and that was the reason for the Brexit: not just the refugees, but the general feeling that the EU bureaucracy does not represent the interests of the people. This was the case clearly with the rejection of Hillary Clinton, where the American population, or at least a large part of it, felt they had no future. In the rust belt, people have a shortened life expectancy—this is the clearest marker that a country is collapsing, when the life expectancy falls!

This is the reason for all of these developments, and also many strategic re-alignments in the world, which I do not now have the time to go into—but it was what caused Trump's election victory.

Mr. Trump has been in office for two weeks, and it is very clear that he is implementing all of his election promises. Some are good and hopeful; others are clearly more problematic. Take his "America First." My comment on the first day he said that—I said "OK, it's fine, 'America First,' but what about all the other countries? They need to be first, too." We need a new paradigm, a completely new set of relations among nations, where we don't have one country being the first but where the new paradigm defines the common aims of all of mankind.

Glass-Steagall

Clearly, globalization was at the expense of the American working population. Because globalization meant outsourcing of industry—the United States has very little industry left, only the military-industrial sector, aerospace, and a couple of other areas. A lot of the productive, middle-level industries are no longer there. They were sent to cheap labor markets. So it is correct when Trump says he wants to bring production back to the United States, especially because you have tremendous problems: you have collapsing infrastructure, you have a huge drug epidemic, you have violence, and for sixteen years you have a rising suicide rate. As a result, he was correct to cancel TPP and NAFTA, because these were parts of the trade agreements of the system of globalization which has gone under.

But what about the effect this has on the other nations? Building a wall with Mexico? Under this system of globalization, the food self-sufficiency of Mexico, which was 80% in the time of President José López Portillo, has fallen to only approximately 50%. So how do you compensate for that? And General Kelly, who now has a new post in Homeland Security in the Trump administration, was absolutely correct when he said, "the Mexicans are not the problem, but it is the fact that all of Central America has fallen under the control of the drug mafia. People are running away because they fear for their lives, kidnapping, drug addiction, murder." Therefore, the question is not the Mexicans; it is really the drug traffic.

After the ban on immigrants for 90 days—citizens from seven Muslim countries cannot come to the United States for that period— there was a huge outcry in Europe, but what a hypocrisy! European politicians felt that they had to lecture Trump on human rights and all of these things. What a double standard! The EU for a very long time has tried to prevent *all* refugees from coming to Europe. In 2016 alone, more than 5,000 people drowned in the Mediterranean *officially*, and that does not count the many uncounted. They are trying to keep people from coming through the Greek and Balkan routes, which are now blocked by NATO barbed wire. The head of the CSU Party in Bavaria, Mr. Seehofer, said that there should be a preference for people that come from Christian Western areas. That is just another formulation for what Trump said, when he said he wanted to keep the Muslim population out.

CC/Mstyslav Chernov

Inhabitants of Suda refugee camp in the Greek island of Chios on the Aegean Sea, seen through a barbed wire fence surrounding the camp, Sept. 29, 2016.

The EU has no problem in leaving the Greek people alone with terrible refugee camps of 100,000 people, who are not receiving much care. They don't care about the refugee camps in the Balkans, where people without enough to eat, and without heating, are trying to survive the winter.

After the very dubious deal with Turkey, the EU just concluded a summit in Malta, where they decided to make a deal with Libya—Libya, which does not even have a clearly defined government—where competing militias are fighting it out, and the EU is now training the Libyan Coast Guard. And even the First Channel of German TV, on a program called "Monitor," said this is a deal with human traffickers and torturers, and competing militias who are absolutely criminal. With these people, the EU is trying to solve the refugee problem.

Therefore, the EU in this respect is not one iota better than the idea of a wall with Mexico.

Trump also promised to implement Glass-Steagall, the banking separation law of Franklin D. Roosevelt. Around that there is a huge fight in the United States right now. It is very clear that the bosses of Wall Street are dead set against Glass-Steagall. They are moving like crazy to prevent it, to keep control. The designated Secretary of the Treasury, a Mr. Mnuchin, has already said in a hearing with Maria Cantwell in the Senate, that he is against Glass-Steagall as it was. He wants to have some modern variety, which basically is exactly *not* what is required.

So right now, we are in a huge battle. Marcy Kaptur [D-Ohio] announced a new Glass-Steagall in the American Congress, in a press conference by Congressmen and -women: Walter Jones [R-N.C.], Tim Ryan [D-Ohio], Tulsi Gabbard [D-Hawaii], who are all for Glass-Steagall. LaRouche PAC is in a major national mobilization. You have many other organizations trying to put Mr. Trump's feet to the fire on his election promise. But this is clearly the Achilles' heel of the Trump administration, because you can have at any moment another 2008 financial blow-out of the system.

Yesterday he made a new executive order, giving to his Cabinet the task of making a review of all aspects of the financial system within the next 120 days. Today, all the financial media were jubilant, saying Wall Street won; the bankers won. Well, it is not yet decided.

U.S. Relations with Russia

On the positive side, Mr. Trump has started to improve relations with Russia. There are very positive signals and that is one of the reasons why the representatives of the unipolar geopolitical faction are so absolutely upset, because they want to have regime change in Russia, and not U.S.-Russian relations. They are now even pronouncing Mrs. Merkel to be the leader of the free world—which is a sort of a joke. Anyway, as to the first telephone discussion between Trump and Putin, both sides characterized it as being very important. This is really a very important precondition, because if Trump had not been elected and we had a Hillary Clinton Presidency, we would be on a short road to World War III. So therefore, this is a positive first step.

But, what about U.S.-Chinese relations? Well, that's a little bit more problematic, because Mr. Trump did not make his first phone call to Xi Jinping, but to the President of Taiwan, thus signalling that he may question the One China policy, which obviously the Chinese government was not very happy about.

On the more positive side, the nominee as ambassador to China, Terry Branstad, is a known friend of President Xi Jinping, and he just attended the Chinese New Year at the February 1st concert of traditional Chinese music in Muscatine, Iowa. He spoke of the long, cordial relationship between Iowa and China, where Xi Jinping and Terry Branstad had met for the first time in the '80s. Friendship agreements of a sister-state relationship were established between Iowa and Hebei province. Mr. Branstad then gave an interview to Xinhua, in which he said that if he is confirmed as Ambassador of the United States to China, he will work for a win-win policy between the United States and China. He added that if the largest developed country and the largest developing country work together, it will not only be beneficial for the two of them, but for the whole world. And that is obviously the truth.

But, where is the potential to make that relationship the crucial change in world history? Mr. Trump promised in the election campaign that he would invest $1

Xinhua/Lan Hongguang

China President Xi Jinping, center, with old friends in Muscatine, Iowa. To the immediate left of Xi is U.S. Ambassador designate to China, Terry Branstad.

trillion in the infrastructure of the United States in the next ten years. He already met the CEO of Alibaba, Jack Ma, and Mr. Ma offered to create a platform for e-commerce of another $1 trillion investment for Chinese investors to invest in the United States, and American exporters to export to China. The Chair of the Foreign Affairs Committee of the National People's Congress, Mme. Fu Ying, recently spoke in New York, where she said the infrastructure cooperation between the United States and China can become a bridge leading to collaboration in the New Silk Road.

The New Silk Road and the U.S.A.

The Schiller Institute developed this idea of the Eurasian Land-Bridge—we called it the New Silk Road in 1991. It was the answer to the collapse of the Soviet Union, and we proposed the integration of Eurasia through infrastructure development corridors. We kept working on this program for 25, by now 26 years, with many, many conferences around the world. We kept enlarging this program, not only a Eurasian Land-Bridge, but to integrate Africa, Latin America, all of Asia into one World Land-Bridge. In 2014, very much encouraged by President Xi Jinping's New Silk Road, we published this report and we called it *The New Silk Road Becomes the World Land-Bridge*.

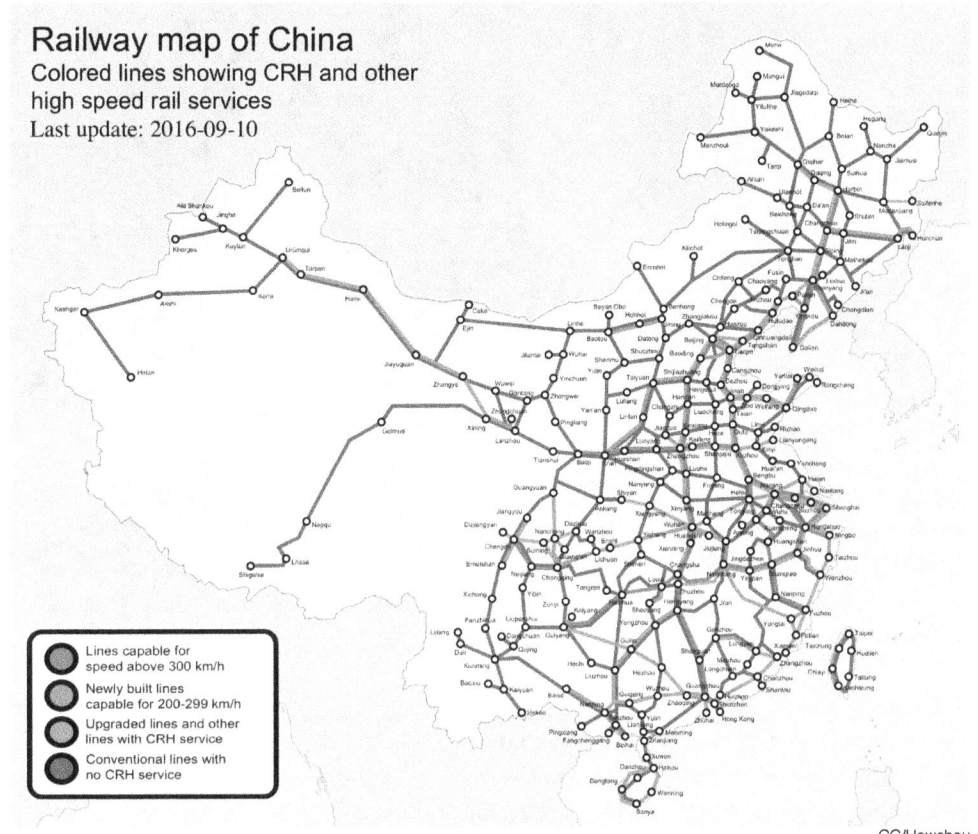

Railway map of China
Colored lines showing CRH and other high speed rail services
Last update: 2016-09-10

Lines capable for speed above 300 km/h

Newly built lines capable for 200-299 km/h

Upgraded lines and other lines with CRH service

Conventional lines with no CRH service

CC/Howchou

Map showing China rail network, including China High-speed Rail CRH (CRH), other high-speed rail, and conventional rail.

system. And I can assure you, having had the good fortune to travel on these trains, that they are *really* fantastic. They are fast and quiet; they don't shake you around like European trains.

China is the world leader right now in such high-speed rail systems. They have a new project by which they want to connect the greater region of Beijing, together with Tianjin and smaller cities, into one very large region, in which people living in the so-called commuter cities can take a high-speed train like people elsewhere take a bus, and be at their workplace in 20 minutes. That kind of a system is needed for the United States as well.

You need to have a new infrastructure of high-speed rail systems connecting the North and the South, the East and the West. Why not build 50,000 miles of high-speed rail in the United States? Then you could combine that with other large infrastructure projects, like solving the water crisis of Southwest America through NAWAPA—the creation of new water from ionization of the atmosphere, creating new water and weather patterns, building a couple of new science cities for international cooperation, starting joint research in fusion power, space cooperation, and just have a completely different approach to the idea of collaboration among nations.

This is where the cooperation with China and other nations comes in. China has already offered cooperation in infrastructure investment in the United States. The United States could immediately join the Asian Infrastructure Investment Bank, the AIIB. And if we use the present motion to implement not only Glass-Steagall, but to implement the Four Laws of Lyndon LaRouche—which are:

In 2015, we elaborated a chapter of that World Land-Bridge report, and we called it *The U.S. Must Join the New Silk Road.* We had several conferences about that subject in New York, in Washington, in San Francisco, in Seattle. We tried to convince the American industrialists, trade unions, and people in general, that it would be in the absolute self-interest of the United States to work with China on this World Land-Bridge idea. [The audio/video, transcripts, and programs of these conferences are available at http://newparadigm.schillerinstitute.com/]

It is very clear that the United States urgently needs a New Silk Road. If you travel over the American highways, if you are unlucky, you may end up disappearing into a pothole. If you look at the number of miles of high-speed rail in the United States, you can't find any. China, on the other side, already by the end of last year, had 20,000 kilometers of high-speed rail systems. By the year 2020, they want to have 50,000 km of high-speed rail systems, connecting every major city in China through a high-speed rail

- Glass-Steagall,
- A national bank which creates credit lines for these investments,
- An international credit system for joint ventures around the world, and
- A crash program for fusion power and space cooperation.

With that, the United States, China, and other nations could immediately start transforming the world.

It is quite interesting. For the last three and half years, since Xi Jinping put the New Silk Road on the international agenda, most Western think-tanks have been completely ridiculous: They have basically been saying that the New Silk Road is just another effort of Chinese imperialism. That they have ulterior motives—just one report like that after the other.

But now there is a change. There is a realization at least among some of these think-tanks, that what is already happening is the biggest infrastructure project in history. What is already happening is twelve times as big as the Marshall Plan in buying power in today's dollars. It already involves 4.4 billion people. More than 70 countries are already cooperating. It is expanding very quickly. It already involves trillions of dollars in investments. For example, there are already eight regular train routes between Chinese cities and Europe, through which container trains arrive every week. As a result, while the EU is still stand-offish, and the German government is still stand-offish, nevertheless there are some changes.

The Vice President of the Federal Academy for Security Policy in Germany, a Mr. Thomas Wriessnig, just put out a paper where he talked about the "Geo-Strategic Significance of the Chinese New Silk Road initiative, OBOR." In his paper, he still reflects a little bit of the old view, being a little suspicious here and there—but after all the ifs and buts, he recognizes the fact that the Belt and Road Initiative has a tremendously stabilizing effect everywhere it exists. Therefore, he basically proposes at the end of the paper that Europe should be open to the Chinese offer to cooperate. And then he says that despite Trump's previous statements that were critical of China, it cannot be excluded that the United States would jump at this initiative and join the AIIB.

Egyptian Transport Minister, Dr. Saad El Geyoushi (left) presenting the Arabic version of EIR's World Land-Bridge Report *in March 2016 in Egypt. EIR Arabic editor Hussein Askary is on the right.*

And given the fact that the United States has leadership in digitalization, and the Chinese have expertise in other areas, these could be complementary, and they could work together to each other's benefit. That is exactly the point.

The New Paradigm

Not only would that benefit the United States. For example, China certainly has better high-speed rail technology than the United States at this point, and China could help the reconstruction of the American economy. But there could be also joint U.S.-Chinese-Russian-Indian-European cooperation, for example, in Southwest Asia. Through the Russian military intervention in Syria and the Astana peace talks, there is the possibility of peace in the Middle East for the first time. But that requires building up the economies of Afghanistan, Iraq, Syria, Yemen, and North Africa, because that will be the only way to dry out the atmosphere for recruitment for terrorism.

Mr. LaRouche, in 1975, had already proposed a development plan for the Middle East which he called the Oasis Plan. This was based on the idea that you have to create new water sources through different technological means in order to have peace. In 2012, the Schiller Institute proposed the extension of the New Silk Road into the Middle East to develop Southwest Asia as a basis for peace. Our World Land-Bridge report has already been translated into Arabic, and a couple of months ago it was presented by the Transport Minister of Egypt in a big press conference in Cairo, together with Mr. Hussein Askary, *EIR's* Arabic editor. Egyptian officials declared that what is in this World Land-Bridge report is also the Egyptian program for the Middle East. As a result, we are not starting from zero, but there is already tremendous motion in this direction.

When President Xi Jinping was in Iran last year, he proposed the extension of the Silk Road not only to Iran, but to Iraq, to Syria, and obviously, from there to Africa and into Europe. The development of Africa is already underway, with Chinese investments in many countries. Just a couple of days ago, the official opening of the rail line between Djibouti and Addis Ababa, Ethiopia occurred. This is a very important intervention which will transform many countries in Africa. China has also now started to make a feasibility study for the Lake Chad initiative, which would bring water from the Congo River to refill Lake Chad, and that would transform the economic prosperity for 12 nations in this region. So there is already tremendous activity going on.

Instead of training a very suspicious and dubious Libyan Coast Guard to keep the refugees back in Africa, would it not make more sense if European nations joined with China and others, like Japan and India, which already are involved in Africa, to develop the African continent?

The formulation by President Xi Jinping, that we have to build a community for the future of mankind, based on a win-win cooperation, is exactly the way to look at this. This is not a zero-sum game where one nation wins and the other one loses, but it is a new perspective where all countries of this planet can work together in the benefit of each. It is exactly the idea that Friedrich Schiller developed in the context of the American Revolution in his play *Don Carlos.*

In the famous scene between the Marquis of Posa talking with King Philip II, in which he said Spain should not be great because of this suppression of Flanders, but should allow all the provinces to prosper exactly like Spain. Posa said to Philip, "Be a king of a million kings!" This was a very clear refutation of the idea of equality of the French Revolution, where equality basically meant, for the Jacobins, that you achieve equality by means of the guillotine, because then everybody is beheaded and everybody is equal. And Schiller contrasted that with the noble idea of the American Revolution that everybody in the whole country should prosper, and the common good should be what unites all.

This is what we have to accomplish today. We need a New Paradigm. That New Paradigm must be as different from the present paradigm of globalization as modern times were different from the Middle Ages in Europe. The Middle Ages in Europe were terrible. They were a Dark Age. They were characterized by scholasticism, by superstition, and by belief in witches. Modern times made it possible to have natural science and Classical culture.

The New Paradigm which replaces globalization must precisely leave the wrong axioms behind, and by wrong axioms, I mean geo-politics, and the neo-liberal idea of wealth creation, which maintains that it is the control of trade, free trade, which generates wealth. It must be replaced by the idea that the only source of wealth is the creativity of the human being. And therefore, the common aims of mankind must focus on this: that what is unique about the human species is that we are the only creative species, and that we can discover universal laws more and more deeply. And we call that scientific progress. When we turn that scientific progress into technology, it increases the productivity of the economic process. That, in turn, leads to a higher living standard, a longer life expectancy, and prosperity for everybody.

If we do this now, we can reach the adulthood of mankind. Wars will be a question of the past. We will no longer use violence to resolve conflicts, but we will concentrate on the common aims of mankind, of space exploration, of reaching energy and raw materials security through mastery of fusion technology, and similar things. If we are guided by such a beautiful vision of the future, we indeed will be able to create a new set of relations among nations.

And I think if we can convince the United States, with the Trump Administration, to cooperate with China on the New Silk Road, I am safe in the prediction that Mr. Trump will not only be a great American President, but that if he can mobilize his country to join hands with China right now, he will go into history as one of the towering giants of all of universal history. [applause]

DR. PATRICK HO

Three Knocks: Basic Questions About Chinese Values

This is a transcript of Dr. Patrick Ho's Feb. 4, 2017 address to the Schiller Institute Conference in New York City.

Dennis Speed: Our next speaker is Dr. Patrick Ho. How can great nations of vastly different cultural backgrounds find common aims by means of which those differences and distinctions are not only overcome, but in some cases turned into new capabilities which benefit the other nation? It is possible for one nation, even for America to learn from another nation, and thereby allow both to improve themselves. The New Silk Road is as much a proposal for cultural growth and progress, as it is for economic growth and progress. As one example of that dialogue, this is our report, *The New Silk Road Becomes the World Land-Bridge*—I think everybody is familiar with it, in English; this is our report, as Helga reported to you, in Arabic; this our report in Chinese.

This report, on the other hand, the 'Belt and Road' *Monograph*, was edited and partially written by our next speaker. It is now being revised. I know some people were asking yesterday and today for copies of it. And those that want them should just see us at the table and we can order them; there's a new one coming out and it can be made available.

Dr. Patrick Ho wrote the preface to this report which is entitled "One Belt, One Road: A New Model of Inclusive Economic Growth and Sustainable Development." His organization, the China Energy Fund Com-

Schiller Institute
Dr. Patrick Ho

mittee has special consultative status at the United Nations and he's here, and he's been here before—he was here in December to give you another talk in the hope that he will inspire us all to do a little work, on behalf of getting the United States, as Helga has already urged, to join the policy and progress of the Belt and Road Initiative. So, Dr. Ho. [applause]

Dr. Patrick Ho: Thank you Dennis, and good morning everybody; it's noon now. I was here two months ago, in December of last year. I spoke on the One Belt, One Road and the most recent thinking about that, and afterwards, I received quite a few questions, not only about One Belt, One Road, but some of the corollaries and implications that it refers to. But all these questions point to one very basic issue, that is: what is the vision behind it? What's the value behind this? And what is it doing to humanity? What is it doing to the world? Is it just a figment of imaginations, or a tic of imaginations of our leaders? Or is it something that's contrived out of the blue? What's the foundation of it?

So today, upon the second invitation from Helga, and from Dennis, and from the Schiller Institute, I would like to take maybe half an hour or so to discuss with you these basic questions about Chinese values. And how does it measure up with the values of the rest of the world, especially with the Western values? And how do we look at it in the context of the history of de-

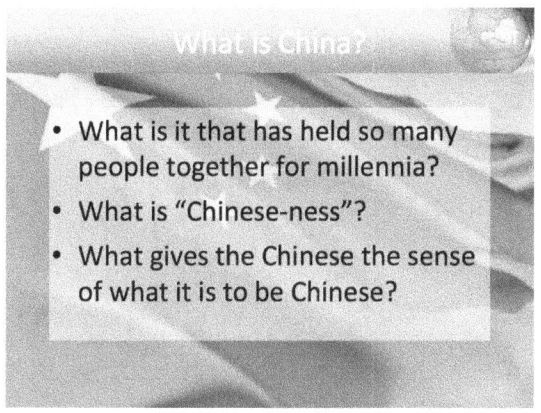

- What is it that has held so many people together for millennia?
- What is "Chinese-ness"?
- What gives the Chinese the sense of what it is to be Chinese?

LAND

PEOPLE

CIVILIZATION

- 3rd largest country
- Longest land border of any country in the world
- >22,000 km
- 14 neighboring nations
- 22% of the world's population
- 8% of the world's arable land

- 54 races
- Diverse, pluralistic, decentralized
- With a common written language & a set of core values derived from their civilization

velopments, especially in recent decades and centuries.

So, we're here today to discuss how the Chinese values, especially Oriental values have influenced the rest of the world. And we will learn from history while also keeping the future in mind.

This is the agenda that I will try to cover today:

I. Presentation of Thesis,

II. History: Overview of the Three Knocks,

III. Yi Jing and Leibniz,

IV: Yi Jing and DNA,

V. *Dao De Jing* and Sustainable Development,

VI. East and West Cultural Core Values: Second Renaissance,

VII. The Third Knock of China.

I. Presentation of the Thesis

What is China? What is it that has held so many people together for millennia? What is "Chinese-ness" What gives the Chinese the sense of what it is to be Chinese?

There are three things you need to remember about China. China is Land, it's a big piece of land. China is People, a lot of people. China is Civilizations, a long legacy of civilization. That makes China, I think. That's my definition.

China is the third largest country with the longest land border of any country in the world, totalling 22,000 km, which is shared with 14 neighboring nations. This is in stark contrast to America. How many neighbors does America have? America has Canada in the north, a weak nation; it has Mexico in the south, a weak nation. It has to the east, fish, to the west fish! [laughter] But China has 14 very *fierce* neighbors, that are trying to steal its borders. That's why Chinese have always regarded the border issues within, always trying to uphold the sovereignty with border issues, with fierceness, with steadfastness, and determination, such as what we're seeing in the South China Sea today. China also holds 22% of the world's population, which it feeds with 8% of the world's arable land.

So, we have heard from our Russian friends, that what they're doing for land would be very, very applicable for China. China has 22% of the world's population which it feeds with 8% of its arable land. So where does the rest of the food come from? We have to make do with what lands we have, unless we get more land. Or we turn more deserts and inarable land, into arable land. And also on top of that, agricultural production has to be of very high efficiency. So we have to have more crops per year, and we have to have more harvesting per each crop. So land is food, and it's economic development.

China, the most populated country on Earth, has 54 races, each with varying sets of customs, habits, and living conditions. It's extremely diverse, very pluralistic, and very much decentralized. They're held together by a common written language and a set of core values derived from their long legacy of civilization. And China is the only one of the ancient civilizations that has been uninterrupted for the last 5,000 years.

China is, indeed, in so many ways not like the West. It is not even primarily a nation-state. Its people are defined by a political identity, but it is a civilization-state, which its people are defined by a cultural identity. Now this helps to explain why the Chinese place such a huge emphasis on unity and stability. Their reference for a state and their distinctive notion of family, social relationships such as *guanxi*, meaning personal relationship, and embrace of ideas such as harmony with diversity. And unlike Europe, China never sought to acquire overseas colonies, but established a tribute system in East Asia through cultural attraction and coercion, never by conquest or by force.

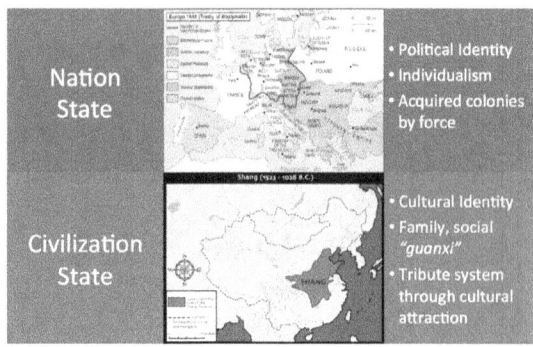

The Chinese state bears a fundamentally different relationship to society, compared with any Western state. The state of government is seen as an intimate, as a member of the family, a necessary good, rather than, as in the Western discourse, a problem, an evil, a threat, or even an enemy of the people. For the Chinese, the state is the embodiment of a civilization and as such, its legitimacy comes from cultural legacy and core values that it upholds and protects.

And in many ways we can already see how the return of China to prominence has not only been good for China, but for the world. By lifting hundreds of millions of people out of poverty, China has contributed to global prosperity.

China's most significant contribution to the world will be intangible ones: It's cultural wisdom, its metaphysics, and its traditional values, a resource unique to China, rare gems formed by heat and pressure over immense periods of time and tribulations. Few if any countries can claim the cultural longevity of China. China's culture is vast and its traditions run deep.

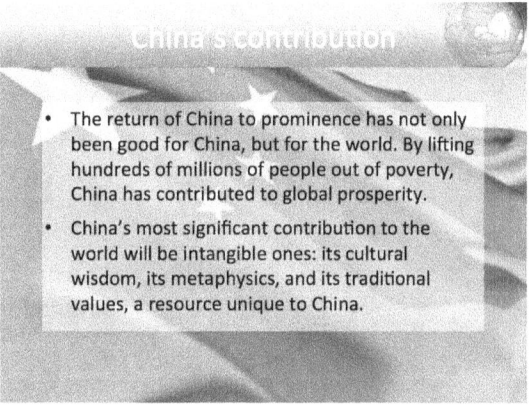

The re-emergence of Chinese culture will therefore help bring balance to global culture. The propagation and exchange of Chinese culture will lead to a wiser more thoughtful and more creative global culture. As it has in the past, exchange will spur innovation, creativity, and cause a flourishing in science, arts, and humanities.

And it will lead to a Second Global Renaissance.

II. History: Overview of the Three Knocks

Just as we knock on the doors and say, "who's there?" in the same manner, we can look at the history of change and interactions between China and the world, for example. Three times

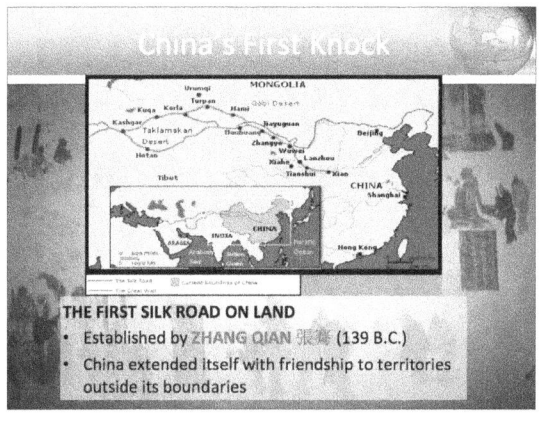

THE FIRST SILK ROAD ON LAND
- Established by ZHANG QIAN 張骞 (139 B.C.)
- China extended itself with friendship to territories outside its boundaries

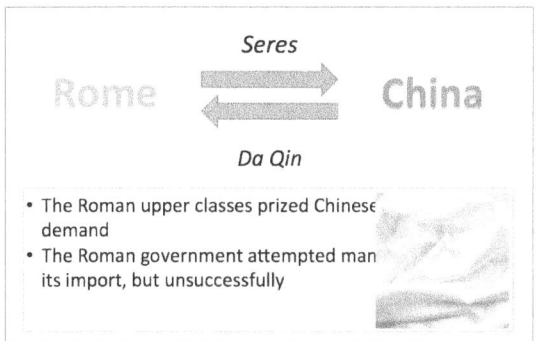

Seres

Rome → China

Da Qin

- The Roman upper classes prized Chinese demand
- The Roman government attempted man its import, but unsuccessfully

Pliny the Elder discussed silk, and its origins in China, in his *"Natural History"*

Gan Ying 甘英 wrote about what he learned of Rome during his travels and discussed the republican form of Roman government

Marco Polo in the Yuan Dynasty, was the best known among these long distance travelers between East and West

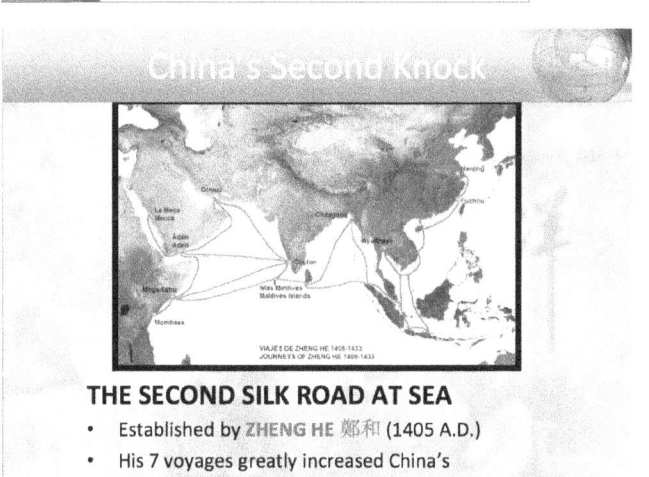

THE SECOND SILK ROAD AT SEA
- Established by ZHENG HE 郑和 (1405 A.D.)
- His 7 voyages greatly increased China's knowledge of the outside world

the West has knocked on China's doors; and three times China has returned the knocking on the doors of the West.

China was among the first countries to undertake major initiatives for long-distance trade and exchange outside of its territories. Two thousand years ago, just about the time of Christ, during the Han Dynasty, Zhang Qian from Xi'an established the first Silk Road. This was China's first knock on the Western door, extending itself in friendship to territories outside its boundaries.

And it was during that period that ancient Rome came to know of China, which it called *Seres*. The Chinese similarly learned of a parallel empire in the West, which they named *Da Qin*.

Among other things, the Roman upper classes particularly prized Chinese silk, with demand so high that the government many times attempted—many times, unsuccessfully though—to limit its import.

The phenomenon was important enough for Pliny the Elder to discuss silk and its origins in China in his *Natural History*. The Chinese envoy Gan Ying, on the other hand, wrote about what he learned of Rome during his travels, among other things discussing the republican form of government that Romans once had. Although limited by the enormous distances, there was already an exchange of ideas between the East and the West, and among the East long-distance travellers, Marco Polo, in the Yuan Dynasty was the best known of them all.

China's Second Knock came in the 15th Century just about 500 or 600 years ago, in the Ming Dynasty, when Zheng He's fleet roamed the seas bringing peace and trade to distant lands. Zheng He was a general and also a eunuch, of the Muslim faith, coming from Kunyang. Zheng He's seven voyages which reached eastern Africa greatly increased China's knowledge of the outside world. Many were the people who found Zheng He's fleet breathtaking and who subsequently sought to become tributaries of China.

In an early example of "panda diplomacy," these nations gave Zheng He a variety of unique animals: ostriches, giraffes, and zebras, among other things. The giraffes in particular brought delight to the Ming court.

Whereas Julius Caesar said, "I came, I saw, I conquered," the Chinese said, "I came, I saw, I made friends, and I went home." [laughter] No battle was fought. No one was enslaved, and no colonies seized.

These two occasions saw China reaching out to the world in peace and friendship, wanting to understand and be understood. We take distance for granted today, and can only imagine the sense of wonder, a spirit of friendship and feelings of discovery that these "knocks" inspired both in China and in the world.

Then the West's turn to Knock on China's door came during the Renaissance, around the time of the Ming and Qing Dynasties. The West's advancements in seamanship, and long distance travelling in particular, allowed it to stretch its influence around the world, seeking trade and colonies under the pretense of preaching Christianity. This was the first knock by the West.

Western missionaries began to operate in China during the 15th Century. Many of these missionaries did not come simply to preach Christianity. They recognized the accomplishments of Chinese society, and sought to learn from the Chinese people. There was considerable exchange of knowledge during this period. The West shared its knowledge of mathematics, medicine, and astronomy; while China shared it philosophies, technologies, and political development.

Matteo Ricci, Joachim Bouvet, and Giuseppe Castiglione were among the many missionaries working in China during this period. Bouvet, a French Jesuit priest, most notably, brought the Yi Jing to the West, where it inspired many. The long-term consequences of the remarkable discoveries that took place in this period, is something I will discuss in more detail in a few minutes.

The first knock of the West on China's door, using Christianity and the sciences, began well, but ended abruptly when the West discovered that the Chinese rites and rituals were finding their ways into Christian practices, threatening the doctrines of the Roman Catholic Church. The door of China was opened for just a while, and then was callously slammed shut.

The Second Knock by the West on China's door, followed the industrial revolution. During this period, Western countries hoping to enrich themselves with natural resources through their military supremacy, forcibly expanded colonialism into the East.

In 1840, Britain, prompted by its opium merchants, invaded China. This was the First Opium War. Despite China's vast economy and its military forces, it lost the war, and was forced

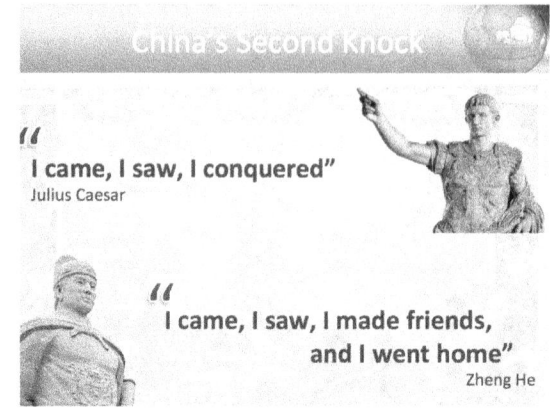

China's Second Knock

" I came, I saw, I conquered"
Julius Caesar

" I came, I saw, I made friends, and I went home"
Zheng He

The West's First Knock

- During the Renaissance, around the time of the Ming and Qing Dynasties in China
- With advanced in seamanship, seeking trade and colonies under the pretense of preaching Christianity

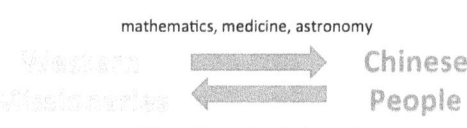

mathematics, medicine, astronomy

Western Missionaries ⟶ Chinese People
⟵

philosophies, technologies, and political developments

- 15th Century in China
- Many of western missionaries recognized the accomplishments of Chinese society
- They sought to learn from the Chinese people

The West's First Knock

Matteo Ricci 利瑪竇   Joachim Bouvet 白晉   Giuseppe Castiglione 郎世寧

- Bouvet brought the Yi Jing to the West
- The 1st knock using Christianity & sciences began well
  → The West discovered that the Chinese rites and rituals threatening the doctrines of the Catholic Church
  → The 1st "Knock" ended
- The door of China was open only for a while

The West's Second Knock

- Followed the Industrial Revolution
- Western countries hoped to enrich themselves with natural resources through their military supremacy, forcibly expanded colonialism to the East

- In 1840, Britain, prompted by its opium merchants, invaded China → 1st Opium War → China lost and was forced to sign unequal treaties → 2nd Opium War & Sino-Japanese War
- 2nd Knock was accomplished with guns and warships
- China's door was plied ajar brutally against her will

China's Responses to the 2nd Knock

- The "2nd Knock" → Cultural and Political Dialogue within China → continued throughout the century
- For China, this process of: self-reflection, self-renewal, and self-fortification
  - Traditional core values have been endowed with new meanings and applications
  - These traditional core values → provided the cohesive spiritual force → bound the Chinese people together during this period of trial and tribulation

The West's Lessons from China

Thomas Wade 威妥瑪　　Herbert Giles 翟理斯

- They developed the first Romanization system for Chinese
- Giles translated the Analects, the Dao De Jing, and the Zhuangzi, and developed the first widely distributed Chinese-English dictionary

to sign unequal treaties with the West.

The Second Opium War, and the Sino-Japanese War which followed—which took place later in that century—brought even more disaster to China. The Second Knock by the West on China's door was accomplished with guns and warships. China's door was pried ajar, brutally, against its will, followed by 100 years of humiliation and national disaster.

The West's Second Knock was a difficult period for China, but it also awakened the nation. China realized it would have to modernize and catch up with the West, and finally began strengthening its military economy and politics. The Self-Strengthening Movement (1861-1895), the Hundred Days' Reform (1898), Sun Yat-sen's overthrowing of the Qing Dynasty (Xinhai Revolution, 1911), the May Fourth Movement, (1919) all were responses to the hard lessons learned during the West's Second Knock.

The Second Knock initialized a cultural and political dialogue within China which continued throughout the last century. For China, this process of modernization has been one of self-reflection, self-renewal, and self-fortification, during which traditional core values have been endowed with new meaning and applications. Ultimately it was these traditional core values that provided the necessary cohesive spiritual forces that bound the Chinese people together during this period of trial and tribulation.

The West itself, despite this aggression took many lessons from China. Thomas Wade and Herbert Giles, for example, developed the first romanization system for the Chinese language. The latter translated the *Analects*, the **Dao De Jing**, and the *Zhuangzi* and developed the first widely distributed Chinese-English dictionary.

The West's Third Knock on the door of China, came in the 1970s, using diplomacy. In 1972, U.S. President Richard Nixon visited China offering an olive branch to China and seeking to integrate the country into the global economic system. When

The West's Third Knock

Feb, 1972	**Jan, 1979**
Nixon's Visit to China	**Deng's Visit to the US**
• Offering an olive branch to China and seeking to integrate the country into the global economic system	• China began its journey of developing a socialist market economy with Chinese characteristics • moderately well-off society

Deng Xiaoping came to power, China began its journey of developing a socialist market economy with Chinese characteristics. With the resulting rapid economic advancement, China became a moderately well-off society.

As with the case of the other knocks, considerable exchange took place during this period. China was introduced to the Western concepts of market economy and international trade. The multifaceted social contact that China experienced during this period was vitally important to its modernization.

III. *Yi Jing* and Leibniz

Now I would branch off just a little bit, and retrace the path of *Yi Jing* and Leibniz. Thousands of years ago, Chinese philosophy found a metaphysical and magical instrument, called the *Yi Jing*, which probably is the oldest book in Chinese history and Chinese culture. It describes not only life and events in the changes of things, but also harbors the secretive and primeval laws of nature. Indeed, Chinese metaphysics is behind one of the driving forces of the present age, the computer and the Internet. These technologies which have revolutionized human experience, can trace their origins to some of the most ancient Chinese wisdom, the *Yi Jing*.

The computer relies on the binary number system to make its calculations. All the activities of the computer, all the information exchanged across the Internet, is ultimately reduced to two numbers, 1's and 0's.

The mathematics of the binary system were expounded by Gottfried Leibniz, a German philosopher and mathematician in the late 17th Century. Although Leibniz had been working on the binary system for some time, a breakthrough inspiration for his work came from China, after he was introduced to *Yi Jing*, and particularly, Shao Yong's work [1011-1077 CE], whose work existed, and who lived in the world some 500 or 600 years before Leibniz.

Interpretations of *Yi Jing* and the Song Dynasty dated from more than 600 years before Leibniz's time. So Leibniz had rediscovered what Chinese wisdom had done some 600 years earlier.

Leibniz was in correspondence with Joachim Bouvet, a Jesuit priest, who among other things, had taught the Emperor Kang Xi, the Western developments in mathematics. Bouvet had come across the *Yi Jing* and had recognized the depth and insight of the work. Bouvet, who himself saw the *Yi Jing* as reaffirming his views on the universal oddities of spiritual knowledge, forwarded the work to Leibniz.

Taiji

Now, there's a series of slides that are very complicated, but this shows you how the binary system and the *Yi Jing* have all

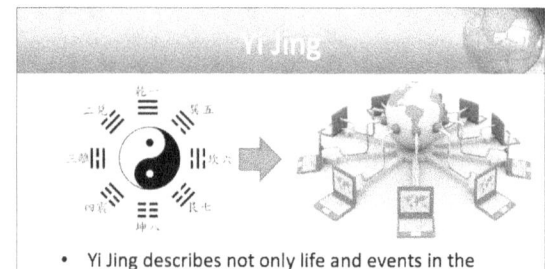

- Yi Jing describes not only life and events in the changes of things, but also harbors the secretive and primeval laws of nature
- The computer and the internet can trace their origins to Chinese metaphysics

The two ultimate numbers: 1 & 0

Gottfried Leibniz
(1646-1716AD)

Shao Yong 邵雍
(1011-1077AD)

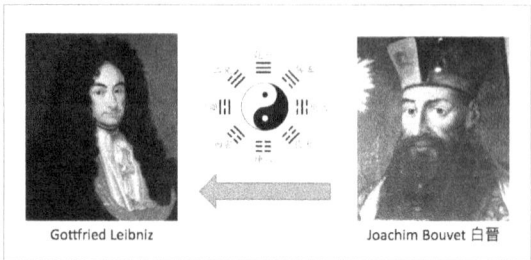

Gottfried Leibniz

Joachim Bouvet 白晋

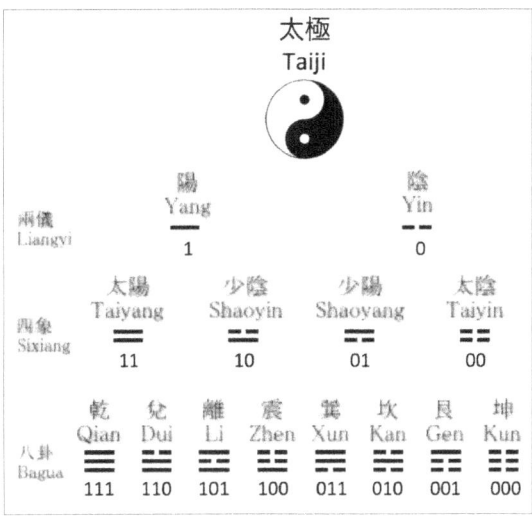

太極
Taiji

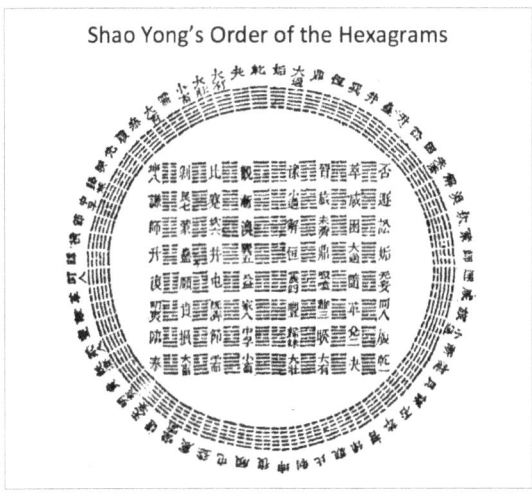

Shao Yong's Order of the Hexagrams

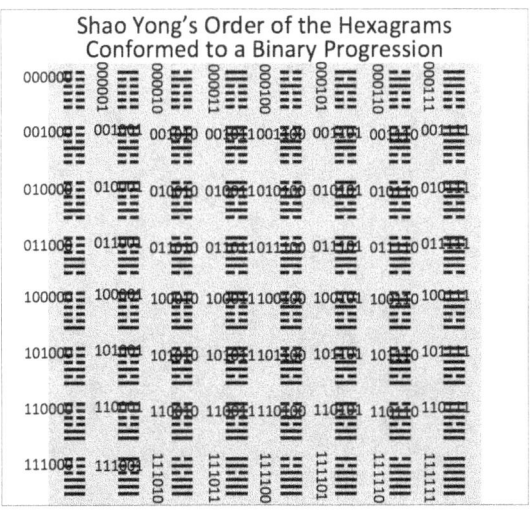

Shao Yong's Order of the Hexagrams
Conformed to a Binary Progression

come together. Leibniz immediately saw the parallel between his work on the binary system and Shao Yong's version of *Yi Jing* interpretation from the Song Dynasty.

Leibniz recognized the *Yi Jing*'s Yin and Yang were equivalent to the binary system. That's Yin and Yang, binary system. [Takes pointer to display] That's *Yi Jing*; this is Bagua of course. Now this is one, what we call a yao [phonetic], this is one yao, just anything; this is yang, yang is a solid line, is a one; yin is a broken line, yao is zero.

When the two come together we call a *Gestalt*, we have two yao together; we have two yin, zero and zero, if you add one to this, is one and zero; zero one; add another one to this and you look at two, but you have 1000 (one thousand) to the yin becomes yang, and then this becomes yin, this 10 (ten). Then you add another one to this this becomes two yang. This is the binary system progression.

If you add another one to this, instead of having two lines, you have three ones, then you are beginning with 000 (zero, zero, zero). You add one to this, you have 001 (zero, zero, one); you add one to this one, then this is bounced by the first position to the second position, so you have 010; you add another one to this, you have 011; you add one to this, you bounce again so this yin becomes yang and this yin becomes yang, so you bounce one of this and it becomes 100 (one hundred); you add one to this and 101 (one hundred and one); get one to this, you bounce this one to this one, so you leaped over one, so 110 (one one zero) and so forth.

This is what is called binary progression; everything from 1 to 9, from a thousand to millions, is all represented by 1 and 0 in different positions. So this is how a computer works. This is geometry; this is calculus. And this is the basis, the foundation of the Internet. This is *Yi Jing*, all right! Aha!

And *Yi Jing* with different combinations of Yin and Yang in different positions came together and it derived itself into 64 possibilities of combination, and with this 64 possibilities, it encompasses all the options of what's happening in the whole wide world. It predicts all possibilities in all situations and all options—all with these 64 of what are called hexagrams—six lines, each line represented by either a solid line or a broken line of Yin and Yang. And this is all this computer, this digitalization.

Furthermore you saw that the *Yi Jing* used those two fundamental values to encompass deeper symbols, assembling the Yin and Yangs to form trigrams and hexagrams. The *Yi Jing* utilized binary calculus and these binaries 600 years before Leibniz treatise of that number system.

And there's another rendition of the *Yi Jing*, the binary system; if you have the time you can go through them and you can see the progression—it's beautiful. Everything works out

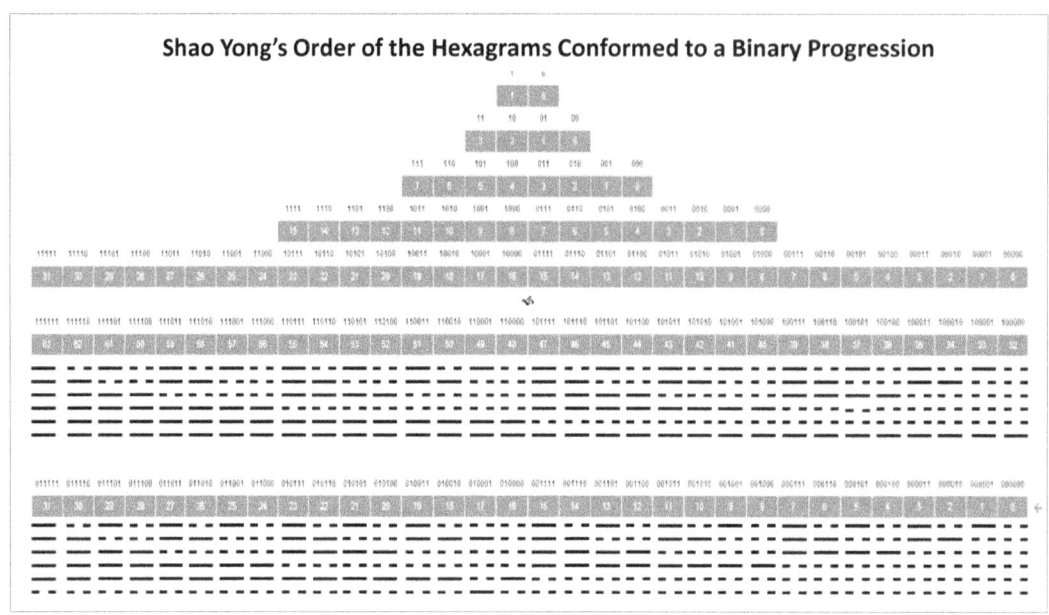

Shao Yong's Order of the Hexagrams Conformed to a Binary Progression

just very nicely, 1, 2, 3, 4, 5, 6, 7… all the way from 1 to 64.

There's another way of realigning this (Shao Yong's Order of the Hexagrams Conformed to a Binary Progression).

Here's another way of realigning this, and this is all binary system and *Yi Jing* (Shao Yong's Order of the Hexagrams Conformed to a Binary Progression).

Leibniz did not hesitate to acknowledge the insight gained from *Yi Jing*, even mentioning the work and the full title of his treatise on the binary system. This is what Leibniz actually wrote in his treatise, and that's exactly the same as the progression of the binary system as enumerated in the *Yi Jing* before. The centuries that followed the publication of that treatise have seen tremendous progress in science and technologies.

This progress has often confirmed the foresight of Chinese metaphysics.

Niels Bohr, a modern physicist, nuclear physicist, and atomic physicist, whose contributions to quantum physics paved the way for the development of the microprocessors, chose to use the Yin/Yang symbol in his coat of arms. And this coat of arms is still being engraved in the cornerstone of the Bohr Institute in Poland.

The exchange between China and Leibniz was the first step in the development of the computer, a technology that now is helping us bridge different nations and cultures. And it could be stated that Chinese metaphysics of *Yi Jing* predicted and lay a foundation for the binary system and opened up a "byte era" typified by computer and cyber-technology leading to a higher level of intelligence.

Gottfried Wilhelm Leibniz
(1646 - 1716)

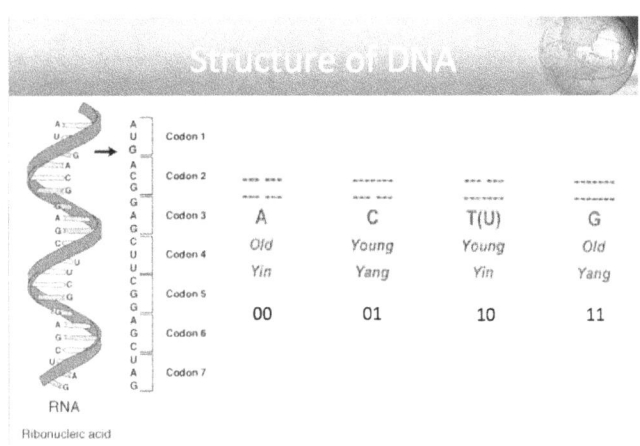

Structure of DNA

RNA

Ribonucleic acid

	A	C	T(U)	G
	Old Yin	Young Yang	Young Yin	Old Yang
	00	01	10	11

IV. *Yi Jing* and DNA

Now *Yi Jing* also has implications for human DNA, and this is the cutting edge of research in Chinese metaphysics and also in the binary system and implications on the DNA. During the last century the strictly analogous relationship between the mathematical structure of this Chinese wisdom from the *Yi Jing* and the very recently deciphered mathematical structure of DNA molecule, was noted.

Now we all know that DNA is made up of four nucleotide-based molecules called A, for adenine; T for thymine; C for cytosine; and G for guanine. These are the four basic nucleotides, made up of all the genes. These letters are in a single long molecule, but apparently they are rooted in threes as codons. That means the possible combinations along the DNA molecules are as such, very complicated but to make a long story short: Our genes are made up of combinations of these nucleotides. Each nucleotide is dictated by the binary functions of what is positive and negative. And you can manipulate and juggle with that, and everything comes out perfectly, fitting the equation very well. I won't go into details because it would take hours to do that.

And this is just to show you that, in modern science, the human body is made up of proteins. The proteins are made up of amino acids; the groups of amino acids are the building blocks of our body. The amino acids are made up of combinations of these nucleotides. The nucleotides are made up of combinations of 1 and 0 (one and zero). That's what it boils down to. So that's the basic elements of the human makeup.

Well, this is 16 already, starting with A, another 16 starting with T—it's very, very complicated. I won't go into this. But DNA is written in words of three letters, out of four possible letters. That makes four by four by four, or 64 possible words in the entire dictionary of the DNA language, called codons, which contains all the genetic secrets of the cell. It was soon referred to a similar mathematical combination and permutation as found in the *Yi Jing*. Both DNA and the *Yi Jing* were based on a binary-quaternary code that generates a system of 64 possibilities for the combination of properties of triplicities and diagrams. Both of these embody probabilistic principles with determination of specific results.

And both systems involve a process of transformation and changes:

In *Yi Jing*: The hexagram changes into another hexagram through the interchange of yin and yang lines.

	dec	A		dec	C		dec	T		dec	G		
A	0	AAA	Lys	4	ACA	Thr	8	ATA	Ile	12	AGA	Arg	A
	1	AAC	Asn	5	ACC	Thr	9	ATC	Ile	13	AGC	Ser	C
	2	AAT	Asn	6	ACT	Thr	10	ATT	Ile	14	AGT	Ser	T
	3	AAG	Lys	7	ACG	Thr	11	ATG	Met	15	AGG	Arg	G
C	16	CAA	Gln	20	CCA	Pro	24	CTA	Leu	28	CGA	Arg	A
	17	CAC	His	21	CCC	Pro	25	CTC	Leu	29	CGC	Arg	C
	18	CAT	His	22	CCT	Pro	26	CTT	Leu	30	CGT	Arg	T
	19	CAG	Gln	23	CCG	Pro	27	CTG	Leu	31	CGG	Arg	G
T	32	TAA	Stop	36	TCA	Ser	40	TTA	Leu	44	TGA	Stop	A
	33	TAC	Tyr	37	TCC	Ser	41	TTC	Phe	45	TGC	Cys	C
	34	TAT	Tyr	38	TCT	Ser	42	TTT	Phe	46	TGT	Cys	T
	35	TAG	Stop	39	TCG	Ser	43	TTG	Leu	47	TGG	Trp	G
G	48	GAA	Glu	52	GCA	Ala	56	GTA	Val	60	GGA	Gly	A
	49	GAC	Asp	53	GCC	Ala	57	GTC	Val	61	GGC	Gly	C
	50	GAT	Asp	54	GCT	Ala	58	GTT	Val	62	GGT	Gly	T
	51	GAG	Glu	55	GCG	Ala	59	GTG	Val	63	GGG	Gly	G

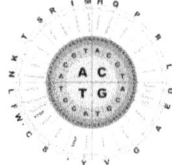

1. Both were based upon a binary-quaternary code that generates a system of 64 possibilities
2. Both embody probabilistic principles with determination of specific results

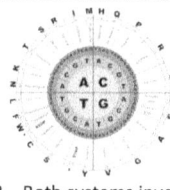

3. Both systems involve processes of transformation and changes:
   - **(Yi Jing)** Hexagram changes into other hexagram through the interchange of yin and yang lines
   - **(DNA)** Point mutation occurs through changes in the nucleotide bases

In DNA: Point mutation occurs through changes in the nucleotide bases.

A very precisely defined triplet of sequences is specific for the protein structure of a very precisely defined part of a living creature. These precisely formulated instructions in the DNA structure define the genetic makeup of the organisms. The sum total of these code words is similar to the "blueprint" for producing a whole living being with all its characteristics. Analogous relationships are gradually discovered to be related to the metaphysical relationship with the genetic composition of living cells. Possibly, such direction of work may provide a scientific basis to explain how *Yi Jing* based Fengshui—or Chinese astrology—may affect people and offspring on a cellular level.

From DNA to Feng Shui

- A triplet of sequences is specific for the protein structure of a defined part of a living creature
- Sum total of these code words ~ "Blueprint" for producing a whole living being with all its characteristics
- Metaphysical relationship → genetic composition of living cells.
- Possibly, a scientific basis to explain how Yi Jing based Fengshui may affect people and offspring on a cellular level

V. *Dao De Jing* and Sustainable Development

Next I will discuss *Dao De Jing* which is another Chinese heritage, and Sustainable Development.

Dao De Jing by Lao Tze, the bible of Daoism, is also a book of profound wisdom and great learning. *Dao De Jing* composing only about 5,000 Chinese characters, 5,000 words, together with *Yi Jing* provides the architectural framework for Chinese metaphysics and indigenous religion. Work has been under way to apply the wisdom of *Dao De Jing* in addressing modern day problems and difficulties in life.

In particular the book may yield clues to a sustainable lifestyle, which is paramount in underpinning all initiatives in reaching the 17 targets of the post-2015 Sustainable Development Goals rolled out by the United Nations last year.

And I'm sure we will be hearing more about this. For example, we know that although with the technological progress today, there's still 1.2 billion people in the world that are still living in extreme poverty. Extreme poverty is defined by having less than one U.S. dollar a day. Whereas 850 million people are still chronically undernourished, while at the *same time* on the other side of the globe, one-third of the food produced for human consumption, 1.3 billion tons per year, is *wasted*—it's wasted!

Lao Tze 老子

- Together with Yi Jing, provide the architectural framework for Chinese metaphysics and the indigenous religion
- Can address modern day's problems and difficulties in life.

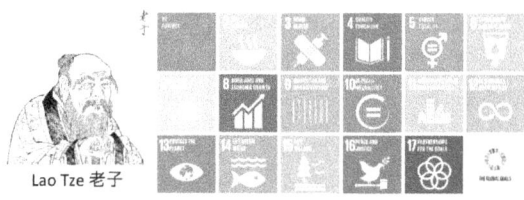

Lao Tze 老子

- Clues to a sustainable lifestyle → 17 targets of Post-2015 Sustainable Development Goals rolled out by the United Nations last month

- 1.2 billion people - extreme poverty
- 850 million people - chronically undernourished
- 33% of food produced (1.3 billion tons per year) is wasted
- 1.2 billion people - no access to electricity
- 2.7 billion people - no clean cooking facilities
- 5% of world population:
  - Consumes 20% of world's energy
  - Drives   25% of world's cars
  - Uses   40% of world's gasoline

- Must inspire responsibility in the affluent
- A sustainable lifestyle:
  use what you need but not what you want
- Careful consumption, use resources efficiently, sparingly, responsibly, be smart
- Against excess and extravagance

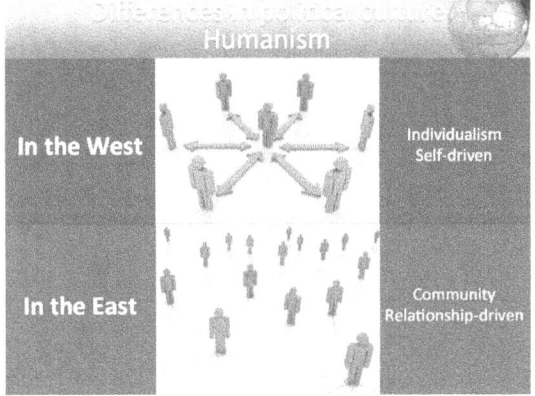

Humanism

In the West — Individualism Self-driven

In the East — Community Relationship-driven

We understand that 1.2 billion people in the world have no access to electricity; and 2.7 billion people of world have no clean cooking facilities. Whereas on the other side of the world, with 5% of the world population,—we're talking about the United States of America—consumes 20% of the world energy, drives 25% of the world's cars and uses 40% of the world's gasoline.

Is that sustainable—Ladies and Gentlemen?

So, a sustainable goal has to inspire responsibility for those who are affluent as well. What we really need is not to hand out fishes, but to teach people how to fish. We need a sustainable lifestyle. What is a sustainable lifestyle? It's to use what we need, but not what we want. There are too many wants and so few needs. So, we're calling upon the world for careful consumption, use resources efficiently, sparingly, responsibly, and smartly, and warn the world against excess and extravagance. That's the spirit and teaching of *Dao De Jing*. You see how we can apply it to the world?

VI. East and West Cultural Core Values 'Second Renaissance'

If we can do that, I think we will see on the horizon, a Second Renaissance. We have seen how the ancient Chinese wisdom *Yi Jing*, combined with the technological know-how of the Western scientists can bring development into game-changing breakthroughs, that deeply affect human life. Such a observation points out the importance of dialogues, exchanges in metaphysical cross-fertilization between civilizations and of different cultural core values.

OK, we were talking about the Second Renaissance.

The Renaissance has brought humanism into European societies previously dominated by the Church, but whereas Western humanism centers on the self. . . . We're talking about the Second Renaissance and this is really the meat of it: What do I mean by that? Chinese culture is dominated by Confucianism. The Renaissance has brought humanism into the European society previously dominated by the Church, but whereas Western humanism centered on the self and emphasized individualism and other specific values, Eastern humanism not only focuses on human relationships which prescribe the essence of a Chinese person, but also the entire holistic makeup in which humans are part and parcel of the overall arrangement.

So this differentiation is not only between the East and the West, after the last elections in the United States we'll see that this differentiation is also happening in the United States. Maybe you can call the Western humanism "liberalism" and Eastern humanism "conservatism." Just watch.

Chinese culture is dominated by Confucianism which anchors its principles on an ancient religious foundation of

Daoism, while establishing the social values and ideals for the traditional Chinese society.

Confucian philosophy presupposes three spheres, three biospheres of human interactions, Heaven, Earth, and Humans. And man must find peace in all three.

For the Man-Man biosphere, Confucius emphasized proper conduct in one's social relations, because it is in the company of others that man reaches his ultimate fulfillment. This code of behavior is called *Li* or the social and ethical norms that guide people to do the appropriate things at the right time, manifesting respect and kindness.

The most important of all virtues is benevolence, called *Ren*, which is love of fellow humans, a sense of compassion based on the dignity of human life and great self-respect. We cultivate *Ren*, or charity, or kindness, or love, by putting ourselves in the position of others and treating them as you wish them to treat you. Confucius said, "Do not do unto others what you would not wish to have them do to you. *And*, do unto others what you want others to do unto you." Benevolence means the practice of these two golden principles which universally permeate all world ethical, cultural, and religious traditions throughout the ages.

Regarding Man-Earth interaction, we are ultimately linked to all life on Earth and therefore must treat our environment with respect and care.

(Differences in political culture.) Furthermore, man's obsessions with development and growth, and particularly still more things to give us greater convenience, pleasure, and comfort, contradicts all teachings against extreme greed, and the principle calling for moderation. Whereas Western civilization often regards nature as an object for eventual conquest, the Chinese treat nature with great reverence and respect. Chinese are appreciative of nature as Humans and Earth, as part of nature, are deemed to be one entity. Such a world outlook brings up a civilization with a sense of tolerance and pursuit of coexistence and harmony.

Concerning Man-Heaven interaction, Confucius honored Heaven as the supreme source of goodness upon which every human being is personally dependent. The pinnacle achievement in life is to be one with Heaven and it is because in Confucian teaching, the primary concern is humanity and the interrelationship between people, Confucianism has only a very general description and mention of Heaven or God, leaving a large amount of room in the spiritual realm for Chinese people to learn from the other civilizations' religions, such as Buddhism from India, Islam from the Middle East, and Christianity from the West. And perhaps, for that reason, Chinese culture, and thus religion, is a very tolerant one, being a culture and religion of infinite possibilities, and capable of accommodating any and all supreme beings.

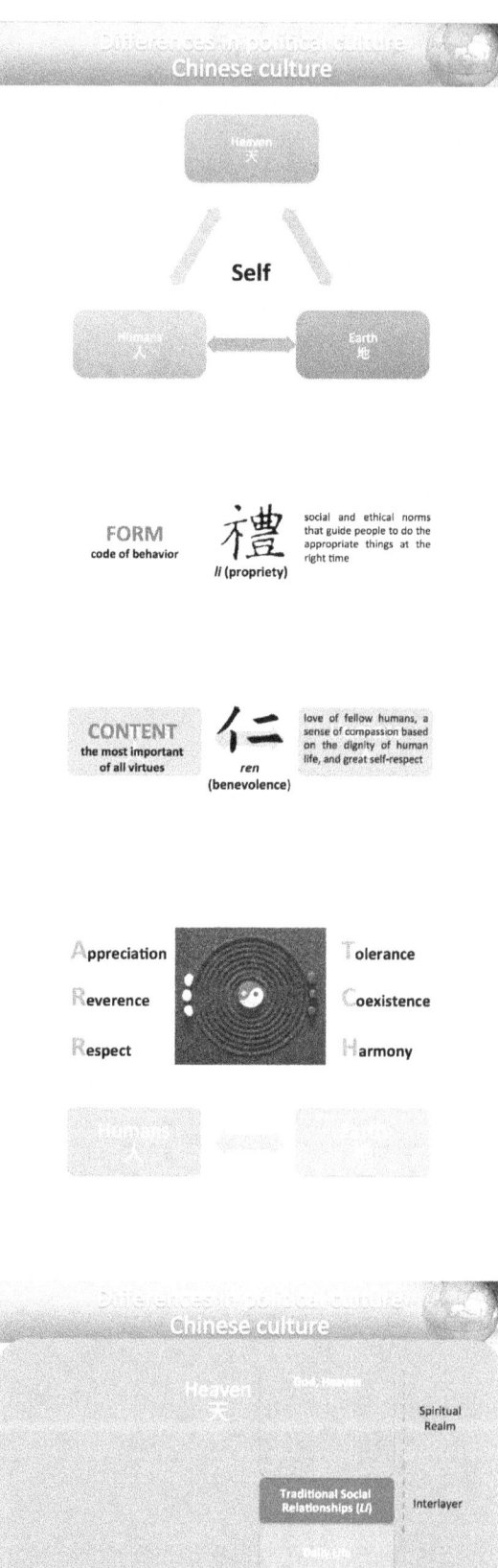

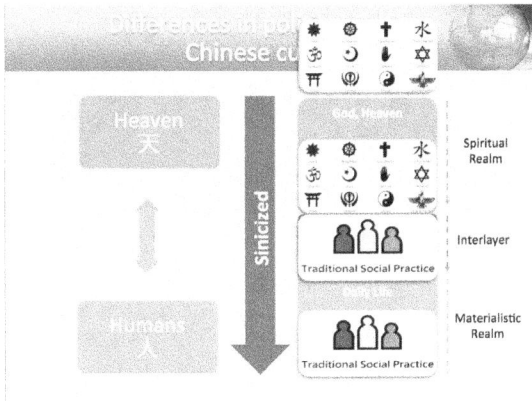

In different eras and locations, the manifestations and the applying methods could vary, but the underlying core values remain steadfast and sustained.

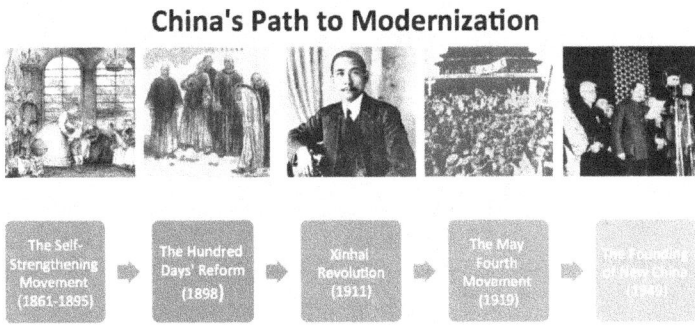

China's Path to Modernization

The Self-Strengthening Movement (1861-1895) → The Hundred Days' Reform (1898) → Xinhai Revolution (1911) → The May Fourth Movement (1919) → The Founding of New China (1949)

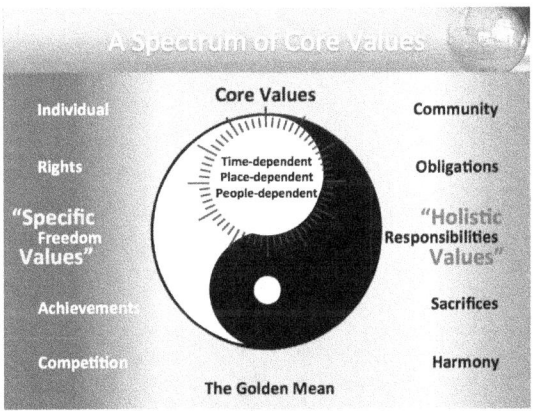

A Spectrum of Core Values

And perhaps for that same reason Chinese would seldom engage themselves in arguments about whose God is the True God and whose God isn't, or whose is the better God. And Chinese culture, unlike other cultures of monotheism do not have the burden of being self-ordained missionaries defending one religion while attempting to convert everybody else to a particular one. Perhaps the Chinese regard Heaven or God as so Supreme and Magnificent that it is beyond description and definition by humans, and that unlimited possibilities in imagination exist with this Heavenly state of mind.

Instead Chinese culture focuses on interfacing layers between the spiritual sphere and the materialistic world, and on which can explain, as a network of social and interpersonal relationships, relationships between man and his inner self, man and his surrounding environment, and man and his fellow man. Therefore, any type of belief or religion can easily blend into the Chinese spiritual world but for it to be practiced by people in local communities it has to be filtered through the Confucian network of traditional and social relationship and be "Sinicized," or interpreted with Chinese characteristics. Therefore, when Buddhism, or Islam, or Christianity was introduced into China, they are customized with local interpretations and have to blend in with the house practices of Chinese society.

So a combination of Chinese and Western culture and Chinese modernization will constitute a Second Renaissance.

Chinese traditional core values are established and time-tested while undergoing twists and turns throughout history.

These values are modified and adapted in different times and contexts, and yet, are made applicable to solving the problems of time. In different eras and locations, the manifestations and the applying methods could vary, but the underlying core values remain steadfast and sustained. According to great learning, if you can renovate yourself one day, do so from day to day and let there be daily renovation. This statement signifies a unique innate quality of a life force of perpetually renewing power of Chinese culture, and gives momentum to self-improvement and self-regeneration as has been testified to in recent Chinese history.

Ever since the mid-19th Century, the Chinese people have been looking forward to a modernized China with a Renaissance of Chinese culture.

We believe that the values of the East and the West are not incompatible. Instead, they constitute a set of values at the two ends of a spectrum, just like the Yin and Yang of Tai Chi; Western and Eastern emphasis of core values are paired to define the latitude of interpretation.

Individual, community, rights and obligations, freedom with

responsibilities, achievements through sacrifices, accommodations with alliances, diversity with harmony, the two sets of values operate with one another as two opposing principles in nature, complementing and supplementing one another. But one will be incomplete without the other. Our decision to lean towards one end over the other in any occasion is time-dependent, place-dependent, and people-dependent. Oftentimes, Chinese prefer the middle way, a position that offers the greatest flexibility, and is called "moderation."

By combining the strength of the East and the West we can make possible a multipolar world order for the modern century. Therefore the Renaissance of the Chinese culture is not simply a matter for China and the Chinese nation. New elements are being injected into global civilization paving the way for a Second Renaissance for the entire human race. This Second Renaissance brings about a new dimension to define and awaken a generation of humanity.

VII. The Third 'Knock' of China

Since the "Third Knock" by the West in 1972, China has undergone a miraculous transformation, blossoming a poor agricultural economy into a major economic powerhouse. The 21st Century will see us embarking on the Third Silk Road, this is the Third Knock on the doors of the West, offering dialogue and friendship, this is a visionary "One Belt, One Road" narrative proposed by President Xi Jinping.

This initiative will help further the exchange of not only material goods, namely energy resources, transportation, and a variety of services, but also the exchange of ideas, knowledge, culture, and values, through new communication lines and networks to promote people-to-people interaction.

The two previous Silk Roads trading tea, silk, spice, exotic fruits, jewelry and gold; the 21st-century Silk Road trades— apart from creative ideas and innovation—*values*. It offers *peace*.

This modern Silk Road travels neither by land nor sea, nor goes from one place to the other, but travels through the inner workings of the human mind, driven by the desire to captivate the advantage of peaceful competition in this globalized world.

In 2013 President Xi Jinping put forward his strategic vision known in brief as the One Belt, One Road Initiative. It is a new model of connectivity among peoples. However, connectivity is not merely about building roads and bridges, high-speed railroads, oil and gas pipelines, and electric power grids. Fiber optics are making linear service connections of different places. More importantly, it should be a three-dimensional combination of infrastructure, institution and people-to-people exchanges, and a five-way multifaceted progress in policy communication,

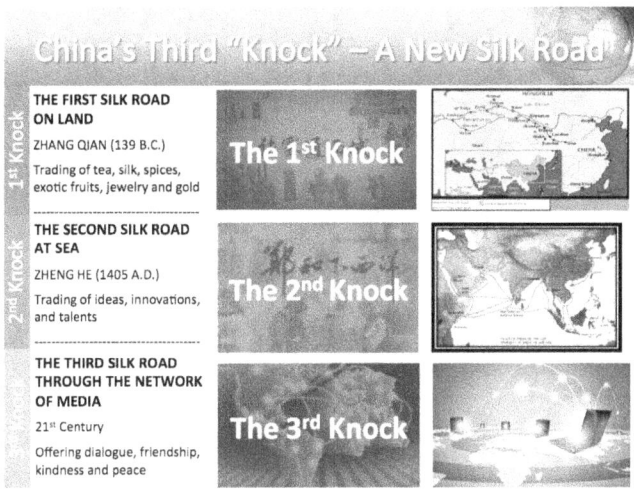

China's Third "Knock" – A New Silk Road

1st Knock	**THE FIRST SILK ROAD ON LAND** ZHANG QIAN (139 B.C.) Trading of tea, silk, spices, exotic fruits, jewelry and gold
2nd Knock	**THE SECOND SILK ROAD AT SEA** ZHENG HE (1405 A.D.) Trading of ideas, innovations, and talents
	THE THIRD SILK ROAD THROUGH THE NETWORK OF MEDIA 21st Century Offering dialogue, friendship, kindness and peace

The 1st Knock

The 2nd Knock

The 3rd Knock

The New Silk Roads
A New Model of Connectivity

A Grand Vision

One Belt One Road

"To forge closer economic ties, deepen cooperation and expand development in the Euro-Asia region, we should take an innovative approach and jointly build an economic belt along the silk road."

Xi Jinping
7th Sep 2013, Astana, Kazakhstan

"China will strengthen maritime cooperation with ASEAN countries to make good use of the China-ASEAN Maritime Cooperation Fund set up by the Chinese government and vigorously develop maritime partnership in a joint effort to build the Maritime Silk Road of the 21st century."

Xi Jinping
2nd Oct 2013, Jakarta, Indonesia

The New Silk Roads
A New Model of Connectivity

- Policy Communication
- Infrastructure
- Understanding Among Peoples
- Infrastructure Connectivity
- People-to-people
- Institutions
- Capital Flow
- Trade Link

The New Silk Roads
A New Model of Connectivity

Infrastructure
- Thoroughfare (roads, air space, ship lanes)
- Railroad (high speed)
- Electric grids (super grids, smart grids)
- Fiber optics (communication)
- Pipeline (oil, gas)
- Water & Waste

infrastructure connectivity, trade link, capital flow, and understanding among peoples.

And maybe even more! It should be so.

Infrastructure consists of thoroughfares, which includes roads, airspace, ship lanes, railroads, high-speed electric grid, fiber optics, pipelines, water, and waste. What are the characteristics of this One Belt, One Road Initiative? Looking back in history, we can learn from the ancient Silk Roads that there were three: Firstly, perhaps people are the most central element. Why is this new initiative for regional cooperation named as a "Belt and Road" instead of group and plan, like the G-7 and Marshall Plan? The answer is, people!

The new initiative is not just a government-to-government (G2G) platform, for people-to-people exchanges. True the process is underpinned by government bodies. But the materialization of this grand vision revolves around people, and it was the many ordinary *people* across the continent that actually connected the East and West together by interactions, exchanges, and trade. Diasporas in neighboring countries could all be mobilized to forge steadfast bonding with the people of all countries.

The second characteristic is goodwill. The second characteristic of this new model of connectivity must be goodwill because this initiative is open to all countries and peoples interested in being connected.

For mutual development, regardless of the forms of government, culture, cultural and religious backgrounds, and geographic locations, common development was once the superglue which bonded different countries along the ancient Silk Road together, and equal footing is what made this "win-win" situation possible—Christian, Muslim, Buddhist, black and white or yellow people, we all benefited equally from trade and exchanges along the Silk Roads.

Western media often refer to the recent rise of China as "threatening." Indeed, in the last 500 years, the Chinese have recorded at least four periods of prosperity. Four peaceful rises without colonies or threats.

As I said before, Julius Caesar said, "I came, I saw, I conquered." The Chinese said, "I made friends, and I went home."

So the new initiative should not be construed as China's ambition to become a regional hegemon, but China's reaching out, offering friendship and peace. More accurately it is also about China's bringing in: Motivated by goodwill, China is inviting people and countries along the Silk Road to build a community of shared interest and common destiny, a community in which no one is left behind and no one has to take second place.

We all have different pasts, we also have a common future to face and a common destiny.

So, the overall vision of the One Belt, One Road Initiative is expected to bring about shared economic, cultural, and social prosperity, but unlike regional cooperation projects which have a fixed policy agenda as its mechanism, the One Belt, One Road Initiative is a grand vision, providing ample and infinite room for creative solutions and possibilities. It is more ambitious and farsighted and, at the same time, more flexible, accommodating, and adaptable to new conditions and challenges than the ancient Silk Roads. It provides an overarching theme and umbrella under which all sorts of cooperation can be made possible.

Simply put, the One Belt, One Road Initiative is neither about seeking for spheres of influence nor striving for hegemony. It is about connecting countries, and people, accommodating differences, embracing diversities, realizing potentials, and enabling various goals and prosperities. However, mutual understanding is the most difficult task in the national cooperation. In fact, it might take hundreds of years for the West to understand what constitutes China, and Chinese-ness. In the recent past, starting in the 15th Century, we have seen the Three Knocks.

The West has knocked on the ancient doors of China for at least three times, and in the first knock we have seen Matteo Ricci, Bouvet, Marco Polo; but the door was shut.

The second knock came in 1840, when Britain invaded China and launched the First Opium War. China's doors were pried open for just a while.

The third knock came in the midst of the Cold War in 1972 when Richard Nixon visited China.

For more than 100 years after being brought to its knees at gunpoint by the West, China has awakened, realizing that it had to catch up with the Western world. When Deng Xiaoping came to power, China

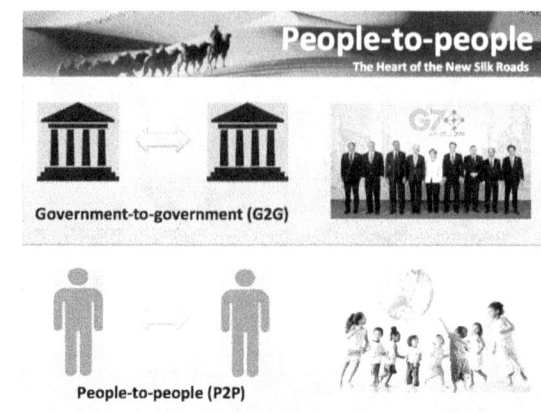

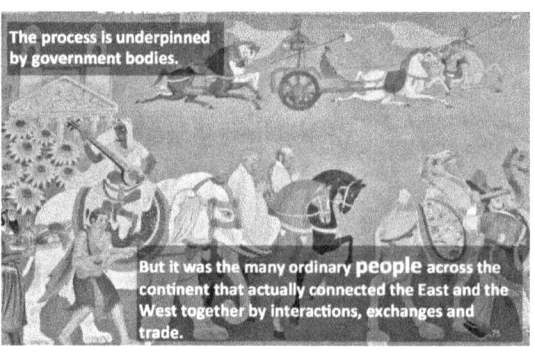

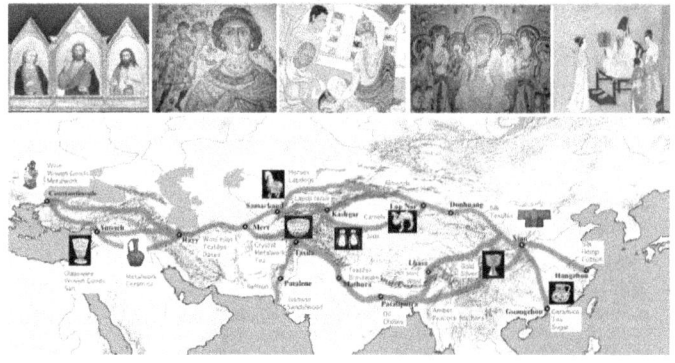

Common Development Equal Footage Win-Win Cooperation

Good Will
The Spirit of the New Silk Roads

" I came, I saw, I conquered"
Julius Caesar

" I came, I saw, I made friends, and I went home"
Zheng He

The Three "Knocks"
The World Trying to Understand China

1st Knock
Priests and Sinologists
1583

2nd Knock
Arms and Troops
1842

1972

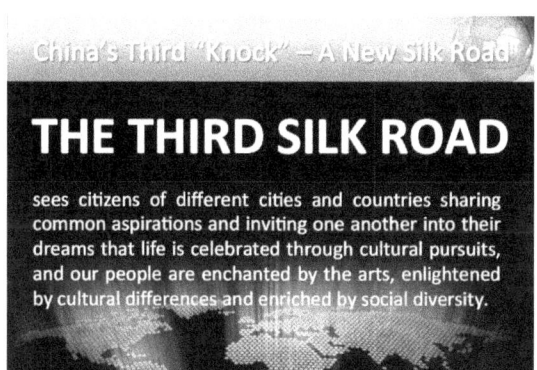

China's Third "Knock" – A New Silk Road

THE THIRD SILK ROAD

sees citizens of different cities and countries sharing common aspirations and inviting one another into their dreams that life is celebrated through cultural pursuits, and our people are enchanted by the arts, enlightened by cultural differences and enriched by social diversity.

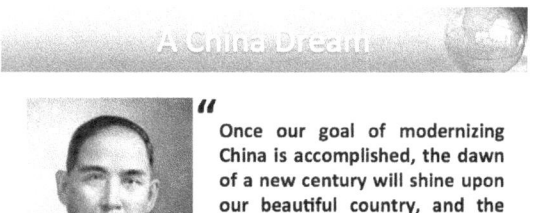

A China Dream

" Once our goal of modernizing China is accomplished, the dawn of a new century will shine upon our beautiful country, and the whole of humanity will enjoy a more brilliant future"

Sun Yat-sen
(1866-1925)

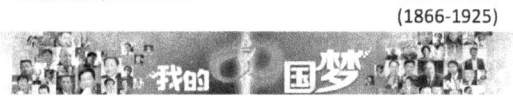

moved, with rapid economic advancement, towards a moderately well-off society.

China's Third "Knock"—A New Silk Road. The Third Silk Road:

This modern Silk Road merges creative markets and aligns policies to form alliances in exploring the commonality among cultures and community values.

This Silk Road sees citizens of different cities and countries sharing common aspirations and inviting one another into their dreams, such that life is celebrated through cultural pursuits, and our people are enchanted by the arts, enlightened by cultural differences, and enriched by society diversity.

This Silk Road teaches people to learn with mutual respect that despite our different backgrounds and upbringings, there are some fundamental values we all hold dear, some basic principles we all respect, and certain core understanding we all embrace.

The purpose of this Silk Road is not to establish an empire of might but to extend our empire of minds.

A China Dream. A very famous Chinese, Sun Yat-sen, once had this dream. He said, "Once our goal of modernizing China is accomplished, the dawn of a new century will shine upon our beautiful country, and the whole of humanity will enjoy a more brilliant future." And last year was the 150th anniversary of Sun Yat-sen's birthday. So we here quote him. And Sun Yat-sen drew his Three People's Principles from Abe Lincoln's Gettysburg Address, and also drew from Henry George's philosophy of man.

Let me take one minute to tell you about Sun Yat-sen. Sun Yat-sen's Three People's Principles, enshrines the throne, and the purpose of doing that is to establish a China which is free, which is prosperous, which is powerful. They say that China has to subscribe to a government of a country of the people, by the people and for the people. Of the people means, Nationalism. By the People means, Democracy. For the people, means improving people's livelihood. And where he got those ideas, he got it from the Gettysburg Address, and from Henry George's "Progress and Poverty."

I hope you all know who Henry George is, right? No? He's a very famous New Yorker. His funeral was the most important event in New York, in the first half of the last century.

Sun Yat-sen got his ideas of national democracy early on, before he overthrew the Qing Dynasty, when he formed the Tong Meng Hui and was first publishing *Min Bao* editorials. But it was in 1906 that he formulated this Three People's Principles and put it in print.

First of all is Nationalism, is "of the people," meaning its cultural identity. What makes Chinese Chinese? Therefore it was Chinese nationalism versus ethnic nationalism, and it's a way of uniting all the 56 ethnicities of China. Not only the Hans, which make up the world's largest tribe, but also others as well.

So he used nationalism to combine China, and formulated a *China nationality*. He was the first one who did that, and even the first flag of the Republic has five colors signifying the five major ethnicities in China.

The second one, "by the people," is democracy, it means "People's Power." He probably separated those into the power of politics and the power of governance.

The power of politics is voting, in the national assembly; the power of people meaning to be able express their political wish and political choice.

There are four powers: Election, Recall, we call it impeachment; Initiative of new processes and new legislation, and Referendum, being reaffirmations of people's choice.

And whereas the Power of governance, is really the combination of the Western three branches of government together with the Chinese traditional administrative traditions, traditions

Three People's Principles

三民主義 孫文

China – a free, prosperous, powerful nation
Of the people: Nationalism (Minzu 民族)
By the people: Democracy (Minquan 民權)
For the people: People livelihood
(Minsheng 民生)

Reference of Abe Lincoln: Gettysburg Address
Henry George: "Progress and Poverty"

1894: Nationalism & Democracy

1905 after European trip (Brussels)
Tong Meng Hui (同盟會): Min Bao (民報) editorial

1906: Min Bao - Three People Principles printed version

Minzu - Nationalism

Populism: people as a nation, independence from imperialist domination

- "China-nationalism" vs "Ethnic-nationalism
- Unite all ethnicities in China (56, 5 majors)
  - Hans (漢): 1.2 billion (91.5%)
  - 55 others: 105 million (Zhuang 壯 16.9 million
    Uyghur 回 11.5 million
    Machu 滿 10.3 million
    Tibetan 藏 6.2 million
    Mongol 蒙 5.9 million)

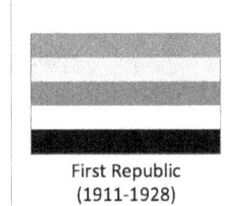

First Republic (1911-1928)

- "National consciousness" unite Chinese races against imperialist aggression
- Minzu:
  - People, nationality, race
  - Sharing common blood, livelihood, religion, language, customs, traditions, culture

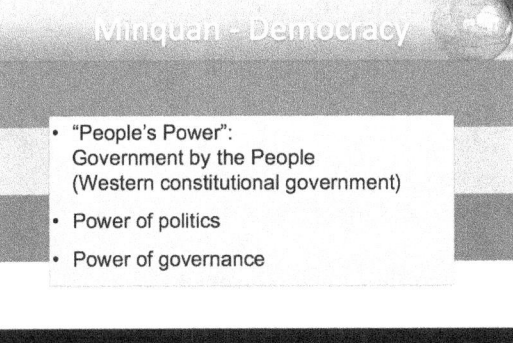

- "People's Power":
  Government by the People
  (Western constitutional government)
- Power of politics
- Power of governance

- Power of politics:
  power of the people to express their
  political wishes →   National Assembly
- 4 Powers:
  - Election
  - Recall
  - Initiative
  - Referendum

- Power of governance: powers of administration
- Combining:
- Western: 3-branch government
  (checks & balances)
- Chinese: traditional administrative tradition
- 5 branches:
  - Legislative
  - Executive
  - Judicial
  - Control (investigatory, auditor, accountability, ombudsman)
  - Examination

Minsheng – Livelihood

- "The People's welfare / livelihoods"
  Government for the people
- Ancient Chinese Teaching

Zhengde 正德	:	Righteous governance
Liyong 利用	:	Create wealth
Housheng 厚生	:	Improve livelihood
Weihe 惟和	:	Harmonious society

- Social welfare: a distinct criticism of the inadequacies of socialism and capitalism (Henry George: tax reform, land value tax)
- Land value tax:
  "the only means of supporting the government is an infinitely just, reasonable, and equitably distributed tax, and on it we will found our new system."

- 4 areas: clothing, food, housing, transportation
- Sun died (1925) before fully explain his vision
- Debate:
  Sun supported socialism or communism?
- Chiang Kai-shek then elaborated:
  Social well-being, recreational needs
- Today:
  Health, food, housing, transportation, education, employment, retirement, welfare, cultural, recreational, spiritual needs

---

of education, and examinations as well.

Lastly is the People's Welfare, this is "for the people." For people in ancient Chinese, good government has to be righteous, be able to create wealth, improve the livelihoods, therefore producing a harmonious society.

For a lot of concerns about government, we're talking about the two—creating wealth for the people, and improving the livelihood of the people. I won't go into details on that.

But I also have a dream. I'm somewhat less known—there's Sun Yat-sen, but "I have a dream. I have a dream of a cultural China, with ideas and values to inspire humanity. The redefinition of Chinese core values signifies the awakening of a modern humanity, and would eventually lead to another human Renaissance during modern times."

As President Xi Jinping and President Obama at the Annenberg Retreat, exchanged views that "The Chinese Dream is interlinked with the American Dream, which is inclusive of the beautiful dream of the people from countries around the world." And what's that dream?

And this Chinese dream is not only the dream of 1.3 billion Chinese over 5,000 years. It is also A World Dream. It is a dream of Peace Under Heaven and the World as One. And this dream belongs to all of us. It belongs to you, and it belongs to me as well.

So, thank you. [applause]

Helga Zepp-LaRouche Responds to Dr. Patrick Ho

Feb. 4—This is a very exciting perspective, but I would actually like to propose, Patrick, that we organize a big event, maybe an international conference, because I think that the knowledge about Chinese culture, but also about Western culture, is really not known to the other culture.

For example, I was in China once, and I was looking for scholars on Nicholas of Cusa, who was the most important scholar and great mind of the 15th Century in Europe. But I only found one professor who was familiar with Nicholas of Cusa. And this is typical, because what you said about the difference between Western values and Chinese values—I think that many times people mistake humanism for liberalism, because of the British influence in the universities all over the world, but also, I think, this has been the case in China for some time. And that is really not true.

We are not talking about the Aristotelian tradition. We are not talking about certain traditions in Europe which then led to certain forms of the Enlightenment—the French Enlightenment and the English Enlightenment—which, as you correctly said, are centered very much on the role of the individual and liberalism.

But that is exactly the tradition which was rejected by what we regard as the positive tradition of the pre-Socratics, Plato, Augustine, Cusa, Kepler, Leibniz, and Schiller.

In science, this tradition includes Riemann, Einstein, and similar thinkers. So there is a much bigger fight in the tradition of European civilization than most people really know. And the entire progress of Classical science and culture comes from the rejection of liberalist tradition. The oligarchy has consciously employed warfare against this tradition, to try to drive people away from the idea of human creativity.

For example, I and other members of the Schiller Institute compared the ideas of Confucius and Mencius with certain ideas and philosophers of the West, and there is a much greater unity. For example, this Nicholas of Cusa whom I mentioned, has conceptions which absolutely correspond to the *Li* and the concept of *Ren* in Confucius. He has this idea—if *Li* is "to do the right thing in the right place at the right time" [as Dr. Ho had earlier mentioned]—Nicholas of Cusa has this idea that each microcosm, each human being, can only fully develop if you contribute to the harmony of the macrocosm by developing all the other microcosms and vice-versa.

That is exactly the "win-win cooperation" among human beings. This is the idea which went into the Peace of Westphalia: the idea that peace is only possible if you respect the interests of the other.

As for Leibniz, Leibniz was so responsive to Chinese philosophy because he himself was a continuation of the thought of Nicholas of Cusa, and he had the idea that each human being is a monad, each human being contains in his own creative mind the entirety of the universe, and concordance is only possible if there is a harmonious development of all of these faculties.

This is what led into the Declaration of Independence and its "pursuit of happiness," which is not "happiness" from the standpoint of luck, but it is exactly the fulfillment, the development of all potentialities which are embedded in the human being. So this is embedded in the human being.

This tradition in European philosophy which we call humanism, is totally opposed to liberalism, and it is much, much more in cohesion with Confucianism than is generally recognized.

The problem with Western books and Western university teaching, is that it has been occupied for a very long time by the people who won the wars, by the oligarchy, by the people who try to suppress this creativity in the population. And I think we would do the next, second Renaissance a very big favor, if we were to organize a symposium to work out these parallels much, much more. And I think this is actually crucial for the understanding of the people from the different cultures.

Nicholas of Cusa said, the only reason that people from different cultures can understand one another, is because they each produce scientists and artists who develop universal principles—and once you have an understanding of these universal principles, you can communicate.

This is why musicians of different nations can be in one orchestra, or why scientists come to the same conclusions about scientific discovery, exactly as you developed with the binary system. I think that there are many more treasures to be found both for the West and to learn from China, as well as for the Chinese people to understand, not about the liberal teaching of history and philosophy of ideas, but to really go to the original sources as they were, and as they were drivers of focus in the West. So, I'm very excited and I hope you can organize something along these lines. [applause]

Why Afghanistan Is Destined to be A Prime Node of the 'Belt and Road'

by Ramtanu Maitra

Feb. 4—For the One Belt, One Road (OBOR) project to achieve what it has set out to achieve—that is, economic development on a foundation of connectivity—Afghanistan must become a prime center in Asia. Located at the cusp of three distinctly separate—and yet integral—parts of Asia, Afghanistan over the millennia has been the corridor through which cultural and trade exchanges across Asia, from one end to the other, have taken place. The same corridor was traversed by many invading armies.

Afghanistan nestles between South Asia, on its south and east; Central Asia, on its north; and the Southwest Asia, with Iran on its western border. China's OBOR has connected the northern part of Asia to the Eurasian landmass through Central Asia and Russia. China is also in the process of linking South Asia to other parts of the world with new and upgraded ports on the Arabian Sea, which will help the OBOR link up with Africa and Europe—China's proposed Maritime Silk Road.

Without Afghanistan's full participation, OBOR could still have access to Southwest Asia and beyond through Turkmenistan and Iran, but then South Asia would remain separated and not linked to OBOR's westward land routes. In addition, Afghanistan's strategic geographic position, bountiful mineral reserves, and other natural resources make it an important nation in intraregional trade and energy networks, both as a provider and a transit hub.

So when a Chinese train pulled into the railway station in August 2016 in the northern Afghanistan town of Hairatan, bordering Uzbekistan, hopes rose. The train

Government of Turkmenistan

Celebrating the opening of the Afghan-Turkmen railway's first section, Nov. 28, 2016. Dancers at Ymamnazar (Turkmenistan) railway station hold aloft a banner of the train. Presidents of the two countries then secured the bolts of the "golden juncture" at the border crossing, to stormy applause.

delivered more than a load of textiles and freight, it brought expectations. That train's 13-day, 700 kilometer journey was full of zig-zags, travelling through Kazakhstan and Uzbekistan to reach the Afghan border. Hairatan—in Balkh province and situated on the Amu Darya (Amu River)—is both a dry port and a river port on the Afghanistan-Uzbekistan border, and is linked to Termez in Uzbekistan's railway network. The extension of the Termez-Hairatan railway link into Mazar-e-Sharif, the second largest city in Afghanistan with a population close to 700,000, had long been identified as a top government priority, and it is now in place. The Hairatan-Mazar-e-Sharif rail link was established in 2012, and since 2015 is maintained by the Uzbek national railway, UTY.

But as a nation ravaged by foreign invasions and a still ongoing civil war of almost four decades, Afghanistan remains perhaps the most insecure nation in Asia, depending heavily on aid money for its daily sustenance. It simply does not have the means to carry out large capital investments until it is made secure. As a result, Afghanistan has no internal railroad network. At present, it is planning to link some of its border towns with its neighbors' railroads, but a fuller plan for a national railway, drawn up by the Afghanistan Railway Authority, is still only on paper (see map).

At Last, Rail Links to Neighbors

On its east, Afghanistan borders Pakistan along the poorly marked and wholly disputed 2,640 kilometer Durand Line. The border was established after the 1893 Durand Line Agreement was reached between the Government of the British Raj (the British Government of India) and Afghan Amir Abdur Rahman Khan, for fixing their respective spheres of influence, in the context of the "Great Game" between the British and Russian empires. The demarcation was never accepted by Afghanistan. It is astonishing that even today, no functional rail link exists between the two neighboring countries, Afghanistan and Pakistan, with such a long common border.

To its north, Afghanistan and Turkmenistan have recently agreed to develop a major rail link. A railroad from Atamyrat in Turkmenistan to the Ymamnazar border crossing point (85 km) and Afghanistan's customs facilities at Akina (3 km) was officially opened on

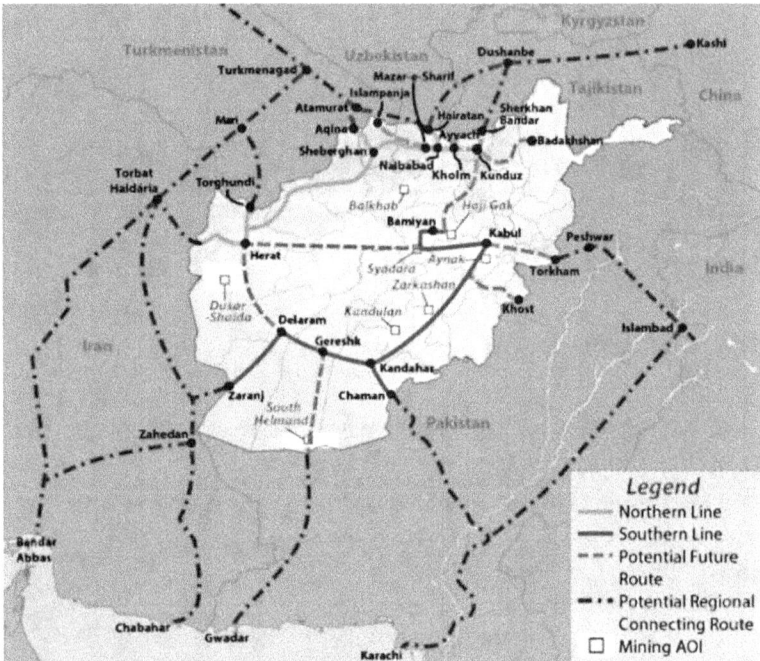

Central Asia Regional Economic Cooperation

The Afghanistan National Railway Plan, developed by the Afghanistan Railway Authority, follows the "ring road" concept. The Northern Line, focused on general freight, will have Russian and standard gauges. The Southern Line, focused on mineral freight, will have standard gauge. Mining areas of interest are noted.

November 28, 2016 by Turkmenistan's President Gurbanguly Berdimuhamedov and Afghanistan's President Ashraf Ghani. Construction had begun in June 2013. This route is also known as the Lapis-Lazuli Railroad, a reference to this historic export corridor along which Afghanistan's lapis lazuli and other semiprecious stones were exported to the Caucasus, Russia, the Balkans, Europe, and North Africa more than 2,000 years ago. Forty-six rail cars of the first cargo train—loaded with flour, grain, cement, urea for fertilizer, and sulphur came to Akina—traveling over two railway bridges along the 88 km Atamyrat-Ymamnazar(Turkmenistan)-Akina (Afghanistan) section.

Plans are afoot to extend this railroad to Tajikistan. That project is known as the TAT Railway (for Turkmenistan, Afghanistan, Tajikistan), which will link Turkmenistan through northern

Asian Development Bank

Tanker cars on Afghanistan's rail line that links Mazar-e-Sharif with Hairatan on the Uzbekistan border.

Afghanistan to the Tajik border. The length of the extended railroad will be around 640 km and would run to Andkhoy, then east via Sheberghan to meet the existing line from Uzbekistan to Mazar-e-Sharif. It will cross the river to enter Tajikistan, terminating at Kolkhozabad on the existing railway from Uzbekistan to Qurghonteppa (formerly Kurgan-Tyube). But this route is not yet certain—variations are being considered.

The Atamyrat-Akina railroad is the second cross-border railway between Turkmenistan and Afghanistan. A short, Soviet-built line goes to a freight terminal at the Afghan border town of Towraghondi, north of Herat.

Looking west, construction of a 191 km railway linking Afghanistan

Azizullah Karimi

Afghanistan's Garland Highway or Ring Road connects the major cities—Kabul, Jalalabad, Kandahar City, Herat, and Mazar-e-Sharif. Much of the 2,210 kilometer road is in disrepair.

to Iran—from Herat to Khaf—is progressing. Herat is the most important city in west Afghanistan, where Iran has made notable investments over decades. Tehran has completed its segment which, from the Iranian town of Khaf (connected to Iran's main railroad), heads slightly south and then east. The line will cross the border through arid and rugged terrain. On the Afghan side, according to local officials, construction work has begun.

By establishing rail links with Turkmenistan and Iran, in particular, Kabul is indicating its priority to link up regionally in Afghanistan's north and west. But recently, discussions have begun in another direction, for a rail connection between Afghanistan and Pakistan. Beijing has shown interest in developing this link, and in May 2016, Pakistani media reported that a survey for a Jalalabad-Peshawar railway (150 km) would start soon, quoting Masood Amin, adviser to the Afghan Ministry of Public Works. Jalalabad and Peshawar both lie near a line drawn between Kabul and Islamabad.

Access to Chabahar Port

In May 2016, leaders of Afghanistan, India, and Iran signed the Chabahar Port agreement in Tehran. Afghanistan is expected to have multi-modal (sea and land) access through the strategic Chabahar Port in Iran, to South Asia, East Asia, and Africa, by the end of this year. Work on the port began last year as a joint venture of Kandla Port Trust and Jawaharlal Nehru Port Trust.

Afghanistan's Garland Highway (or Ring Road) can be reached from Chabahar Port using the existing Iranian road network and the Zaranj-Delaram road, constructed by India in 2009. The road connects Zaranj on the Iran border with the Ring Road at Delaram.

Now on the drawing boards is a rail link between Chabahar Port and Zahedan (Iran), close to the intersection of the Iran, Afghanistan, and Pakistan borders and about 200 km from Zaranj. The Indian state-owned IRCON has an agreement with the Construction, Development of Transport, and Infrastructure Company (CDTIC) of Iran to build the link at a cost of $1.6 billion, as part of the transit corridor to Afghanistan.

A Ring Road in Poor Repair

With no railway network that criss-crosses and unites Afghanistan, efficient movement within the country depends entirely on the 2,210 km Ring Road, a highway that lies inside Afghanistan like a garland. It is the only transport system that not only connects many Afghans within the country, but also connects with Pakistan, Tajikistan, and Iran.

Construction of the Ring Road began in Herat province bordering Iran. From there it goes south, passing through Nimruz, Farah, and Helmand provinces before reaching Kandahar. The road continues through the eastern provinces of Zabul, Ghazni, Wardak, Kabul, and Parwan. It then passes through Baghlan to reach

Balkh in the north. From Balkh province, which borders Uzbekistan, it turns west through Jowzjan, Faryab, and Badghis provinces before returning to Herat and completing the garland. But the last segment, connecting Akina on the Turkmenistan border with Herat, still has 233 km of road missing. There are some entirely unpaved stretches of dirt track.

The ongoing armed conflict engulfing most of Afghanistan has significantly damaged the condition of the Ring Road and the regional road networks. The U.S. Special Inspector General for Afghanistan Reconstruction (SIGAR), John Sopko, in his October 2016 report, pointed out that the billions of dollars spent by USAID and the U.S. Department of Defense have done little to restore the full functionality of these roads. He wrote,

> SIGAR selected and assessed the condition of 1,640 kilometers of U.S.-funded national and regional highways, or approximately 22 percent of all paved roads in Afghanistan. The results indicate that most of these highways need repair and maintenance. For example, SIGAR performed inspections of 20 road segments and found that 19 segments had road damage ranging from deep surface cracks to roads and bridges destroyed by weather or insurgents. Moreover, 17 segments were either poorly maintained or not maintained at all, resulting in road defects that limited drivability. MOPW [Ministry of Public Works] officials acknowledged that roads in Afghanistan are in poor condition. In August 2015, an MOPW official stated that 20 percent of the roads were destroyed and the remaining 80 percent continue to deteriorate. The official added that the Kabul to Kandahar highway is beyond repair and needs to be rebuilt. USAID estimated that unless maintained, it would cost about $8.3 billion to replace Afghanistan's road infrastructure, and estimated that 54 percent of Afghanistan's road infrastructure suffered from poor maintenance and required rehabilitation beyond simple repairs.

A Transportation Network Is Crucial

Afghanistan has very difficult terrain. Larger than France, but with less than half of France's population, it is dominated by the Hindu Kush mountain range and its extending ranges to the west. The 800 km (500 mile) Hindu Kush descends to the valley of the Amu Darya

CC/Todd Huffman
On the road from Kabul to Jalalabad, toward Pakistan.

on the north and the Indus River valley on the south. The Hindu Kush straddles the Pakistan-Afghanistan frontier and crosses Afghanistan in a generally southwestward direction, gradually diminishing in altitude until, opposite Kabul (and to its west), the main ridge is from 15,000 to 20,000 feet high. One hundred miles or so northwest of Kabul, the Koh-i-Baba range—overlapping the western extremity of the Hindu Kush with which it is connected by the Shibar Pass—prolongs the watershed to the west past Bamiyan. On the northeastern side of the Hindu Kush—

> Round the Kunar Valley and in Nuristan, the deep ravines and precipitous slopes are clad with magnificent forests of deodar, pine and larch. Further west the slopes and ridges are bare and brown. In the narrow valleys where the swift-running streams, snow-fed from the peaks above, make irrigation possible. Although in some high valleys are to be found stretches of grasslands, the general impression of the great range is of a wild, desolate little-known country, a country of great peaks and deep valleys, of precipitous gorges and rushing grey-green rivers. (W.K. Fraser-Tytler, *Afghanistan: A study of Political Developments in Central and Southern Asia*, 1950)

So wrote a historian who traveled through Afghanistan. Only a transport network can unite such a land.

The Many Peoples

These natural barriers created by the Hindu Kush range, and the lack of transportation networks, have kept Afghanistan's ethnic groups as varied as ever. The Pushtuns, whose original home in the region was the Suleiman Range on the eastern border of Pakistan's Balochistan province, have their own language, Pushtu. Although it is difficult to pin down their origin, it is likely they are of Turko-Iranian stock with a generous admixture of Indian blood. Among them are the Ghilzais, a large community among the Pushtuns.

CC/Steve Evans

The Blue Mosque of Mazar-e-Sharif, where Ali bin Abi Talib, son-in-law of the prophet Muhammad and founder of Shi'a Islam, is interred.

Some historians claim the Ghilzais are of Turkish stock and were pre-eminently a nomad people grazing sheep and cattle, who moved from one grazing pasture to another seasonally. Hundreds of years ago they were pre-eminent in the Kabul and Ghazni areas, but more recently they have spread southwards.

In the north, Tajiks, a non-nomad people of Persian origin, and the Uzbeks, of Turkish origin, dominate. The Tajiks are settled mostly around Kabul, in Kohistan and the valley of the Panjshir River, and in the northeast beyond the Hindu Kush in the valley of upper Amu Darya. Uzbeks are found all along the plains from Murghab River on the west to Faizabad in the Badakhshan province in the east. They are farmers and breed Turkmen horses and the famous Karakul sheep. There is also a small community of Turkmen along the south-

ern bank of the Amu Darya. There are Kyrgyz living on the upper reaches of Amu Darya, in the narrow Wakhan corridor that ends at the border with China's Xinjiang province. Their ancestors probably migrated from eastern Siberia.

Several hundred thousand Nuristanis live at high elevations along small river valleys in northeast Afghanistan, along the border with Pakistan, north of Kabul and Jalalabad and south of the Wakhan corridor. The Nuristanis believe they are either related to the Greek occupying forces of Alexander of Macedon that invaded the region in about 330 BCE, or to the tribes of Mecca who rejected Islam.

In Afghanistan's west, known as the Hazarajat, live the descendants of Tatar regiments brought to Afghanistan by Chinggis Khan. The Tatars are a result of the combination of ethnicities that allied with Chinggis Khan's Mongols in their wars across Eurasia. The Hazaras, a large community, most of whom are Twelver Shi'a, are also found in Baghlan, Samangan, Balkh, Jawzjan, and Badghis provinces. There are close to 750,000 Hazaras living in Afghanistan and almost a million spread over Iran and Pakistan. Hazaras have a very strong presence in Central Afghanistan, living in pastoral lands situated among narrow valleys, rugged mountain slopes, and turbulent rivers.

The dispersion of cultures cries out for a transportation network, to enable the peoples to become participants in a single nation.

rightnow.org.au

Hazara family in Afghanistan. The Hazaras are descended from Tatar regiments of Chinggis Khan. Note indication of tillage, upper left.

Mineral Extraction Awaits Stability

In addition to inadequate transportation, the organized opium cultivation that profits many, from bankers to bandits, has turned Afghanistan into a center of permanent conflict and insecurity. Thousands of tons of opium are produced annually under the watch of thousands of NATO troops. The cash generated from opium cultivation not only feeds the world's cash-short banks and other vultures, but provides insurgents with arms and cash to carry out destruction and prolong Afghanistan's instability. Unless this menace is completely eradicated, OBOR, or any other plan to build up Afghanistan, will have no effect whatever. On the other hand, once Afghanistan is stabilized, it could become a truly prosperous nation, while playing a major role as the hub and meeting point of Central Asia, South Asia, and Southwest Asia in the China-led OBOR.

Afghanistan Ministry of Mines

Afghanistan's largest copper deposit is here at Mes Aynak, near Kabul.

Unlike many Central Asian nations, but like South Asian nations, Afghanistan is not an oil producing country. The country imports petroleum products such as diesel, gasoline, and jet fuel from Pakistan and Uzbekistan, with limited volumes from Turkmenistan and Iran. But Afghanistan is rich in mineral wealth and also has the potential to become an exporter of agricultural products. U.S. hydrologists and mining engineers are working with Afghans southeast of Kabul in conducting tests to determine where mining is feasible. It could take up to 10 years for new mine operations to be established. The deposits are mainly of copper, but also include gold, iron ore, uranium, and precious stones such as emeralds.

Afghanistan's Mes Aynak site, 40 km southeast of Kabul, reportedly has $100 billion in copper resources underground. In 2008 Kabul awarded a 30-year concession for mining to MCC, a Chinese joint venture. The copper mine development will produce annually approximately 200,000 tons of copper cathode or an equivalent amount of copper concentrate. MCC proposed to build a coal-fired power plant and supply 50 per cent of the power generated to Kabul and the surrounding community, and build a railroad to Xinjiang. Kabul considers Mes Aynak, which is expected to generate about 7,000 jobs, to be a crucial project. Mes Aynak also offers the opportunity to serve as a major anchor project for the development of upstream, downstream, and side-stream linkages as well as ancillary infrastructure that will drive economic growth. The project, however, has not taken off.

Mes Aynak is host to a trove of archeological ruins in a settlement that includes Buddhist statues, stupas (shrines), and a monastery complex dating from the time of the ancient Silk Road, when this area was a part of Gandhara. Gandhara provided major cultural impulses eastward along the Silk Road, including Greco-Buddhist sculptural styles. The settlement reached the peak of its prosperity in the fifth century CE. There are also remains at a lower level that date to the Bronze Age, about 3,000 BCE. International efforts are afoot to prevent or greatly delay the exploitation of the copper deposits, which would destroy any remains that had not been rescued. The motivation, however, is a combination of bad and good intentions.

Another major mining project that is yet to take off is the plan for an iron ore mine at Hajigak in Bamiyan Province, west of Kabul. Hajigak is the largest iron ore oxide deposit in Afghanistan—with 1.8 billion metric tons of ore—and is also Asia's largest untapped iron ore deposit. Seven of its 16 zones have been studied in detail. While concessions have been discussed with the Indian consortium SAIL-Affisco, consisting of seven companies with support from India's government, contracts have not been signed and no work is underway in Hajigak.

Stability is a key to progress in mining.

Eradicate Opium, Modernize Agriculture

Wheat is Afghanistan's most important crop, followed by barley, corn, and rice, grown mostly in the northern plains, a region that extends eastward from the Iranian border to the foothills of the Pamir mountain range near the Tajikistan border. Cotton is another important and widely cultivated crop. Fruit and nuts are among Afghanistan's most important exports. Afghanistan is noted for its unusually sweet grapes and melons, grown mostly in the southwest, north of the Hindu Kush, and in the fertile regions around Herat. Raisins are also an important export. Other important fruits are apricots, cherries, figs, mulberries, and pomegranates. However, the absence of adequate irrigation networks, and the lack of dams and reservoirs to facilitate such irrigation networks, has limited Afghanistan's agriculture. Because of the lack of dams and reservoirs, much of the water flows into neighboring countries or is wasted in the deserts.

In the southern part of the country, where desert-like plains abut Iran, an extensive railroad network can be developed to facilitate transport between agricultural lands and urban centers. A well-fed population will be more healthy and productive and, over the years, will be capable of greater diversity in its pursuit of future options. The agricultural sector will require agro-machinery such as tractors, harvesters, and hoeing machines. The manufacturing and maintenance of such machinery will introduce industries that will train skilled workers and technicians.

Agriculture to Build the Nation

The most fundamental benefit of a successful, modern agricultural sector lies in what it builds into the nation. Such an agricultural sector requires power, water, sufficient manpower, development of agro-industries, and a transportation network throughout the country. A successful agricultural sector needs concerted effort, and if the importance of the agricultural sector is fully understood, and developed in depth, it provides a shield against external manipulation. The process itself develops skilled manpower.

Basic agricultural institutions include research and extension services that create agronomists who live in the country, work to develop high-yield varieties of seeds, and improve undernourished land. Development of water resources—including irrigation and water supply for the agro-industries and the population in general—produces engineers and technicians who build dams, canals, and flood plains. These actions themselves protect the soil, the land, and the environment in general.

Ramtanu Maitra is the author of many analyses of South and Central Asia, including "Long-Term Planning for a Post-War Afghanistan," Executive Intelligence Review, *Aug. 13, 2010.*

War of Extermination In Yemen Accelerates

by Ulf Sandmark

Feb. 3—The ongoing genocide in the Yemen civil war is now the worst humanitarian crisis in the world, according to the UN Office for the Coordination of Humanitarian Affairs (OCHA). The blockade of the country has drastically reduced imports of food, fuel, and medicines, while roads and bridges, dams, hospitals, schools, and markets are being systematically bombed. Twelve percent of the population is now suffering from "acute malnutrition"—3.3 million of Yemen's 28 million.

The UN Security Council (UNSC) is also implicated, in that UNSC Resolution 2216 violates the UN Charter by putting blame exclusively on one party in a domestic conflict.

The years of malnutrition are now beginning to take their devastating toll. Civilian deaths from the war were estimated at 11,403 in November 2016 after 20 months of bombing. Now deaths from starvation have far overtaken the direct war casualties. UNICEF reported Jan. 31 that 63,000 Yemeni children had died during 2016 of malnutrition; the report does not give a figure for the adult deaths. Almost half a million children are now in a state of "severe acute malnutrition," that is, they are about to die. Overall, 3.3 million Yemenis, 2.2 million of whom are children, are suffering from "acute malnutrition."

Currently 14 million people (half of the population) are "food insecure," of whom half are "severely food insecure." This means that at least 7 million people need emergency food assistance to survive.

UN Security Council Inaction

Having disregarded the Yemen crisis since October 2016, the UNSC received a briefing on Jan. 26 from the UN Office for Coordination of Humanitarian Affairs (OCHA), on the initiative of the Swedish chairmanship of the UNSC, according to a source close to the Swedish government. The genocide has so far been played down at the UN in general. The OCHA report indicated that the Yemen genocide is accelerating and that it is the worst humanitarian crisis in the world now.

The UNSC discussed the possibilities of opening the airport and Houdeida harbor for emergency human-

CC/Ibrahem Qasim

Destroyed house in the south of Sana'a.

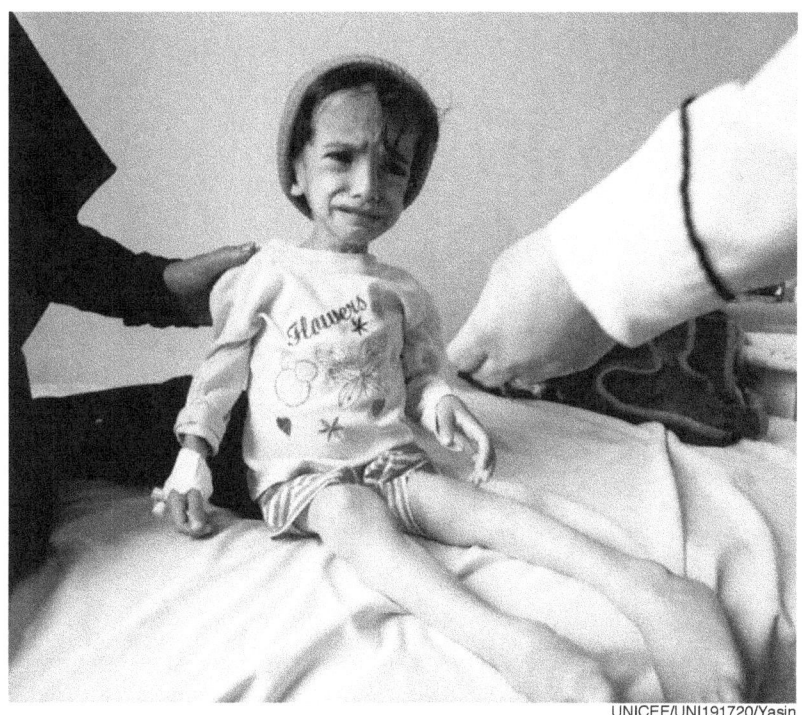

UNICEF/UNI191720/Yasin

A malnourished 2-year-old girl receiving treatment at a hospital in Sana'a.

must write any amendment. In the language of *Security Council Report*, a watchdog independent of the UNSC, "As the penholders take the lead in drafting Council decisions, they normally 'trump' chairs, notwithstanding the formal title and mandate of the latter."

Denying Food, Bombing Schools

There are many tricks in the implementation of the resolution that have to be exposed. One such trick is that most imports of food, medicine, and fuel are stopped even before they leave the harbor of origin, as an application for import permission has to be approved. It is almost never accepted. The application goes to the Yemeni transport ministry of the Hadi government now in Riyadh, which rejects it, blocking imports to the North. Even humanitarian assistance has difficulty in getting permission.

The Hadi government is in physical control of Aden, the other big harbor in Yemen, but the Aden harbor is highly insecure because of proliferating, undisciplined militias and outright terrorist bands, such as Al-Qaeda in the Arabian Peninsula (AQAP) and Daesh (ISIS). The UN relief organizations cannot

itarian assistance. There are 20,000 people waiting to go abroad for specialized medical treatment. The Sana'a airport, closed because it has been bombed, is also important for bringing in journalists, as it is almost impossible to travel to Yemen now and very little independent news comes out. The only harbor under the control of the Sana'a government, Houdeida, is blockaded from the sea. The harbor's cranes were bombed by the Saudis, who support president-in-exile Abd Rabbuh Mansur Hadi. Four new mobile cranes, brought by the World Food Program, are not being allowed to land and are waiting aboard ship at sea.

But there is no new resolution—or amendment to Resolution 2216—in the pipeline, according to the source. The British are the UNSC "penholder" for this issue, which means that the British UN representatives are the ones who

UN Ocha/Charlotte Cans

Abdallah Mohamed Al Qady stands in what had been the entrance of his family home in Bayt Mayad neighbourhood of Sana'a, Yemen. The four-storey house was completely destroyed when a missile landed next door on June 13, 2015.

bring food ashore there, and it remains in the ships or in Djibouti, across the Gulf.

The bombing war is illegal as it perpetrates war crimes against Yemen by systematically attacking (1) civilian targets such as homes, hospitals, schools, markets, and funerals; (2) food procurement, the harbor, roads and bridges, fuel and food storage facilities, food production, and dams; (3) ancient cultural heritage sites, museums, cities, mosques— collectively, a world treasure. The bombing has even made farm fields unusable with cluster bombs that disperse mines.

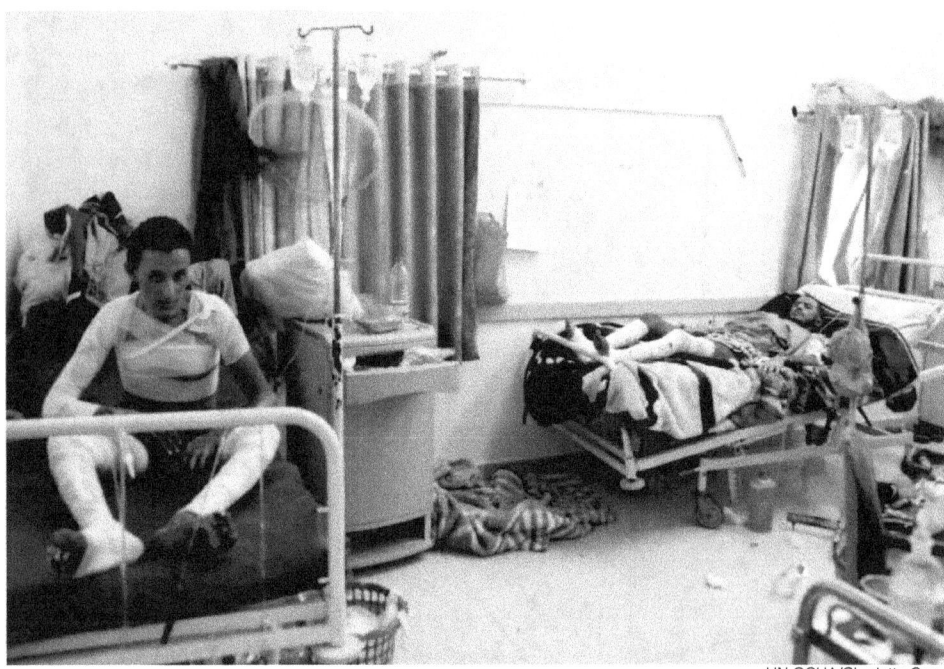
UN OCHA/Charlotte Cand

Adam Abdullah (20 years old, left) and Youssouf Harban (24 years old, right) at Jumhouri hospital in Sana'a. Adam was injured when an air strike hit his house in Sa'ada. Youssouf was wounded when an air strike hit a market in Sa'ada.

The U.K. Ministry of Defence has noted 252 alleged violations of international law by the Saudi-led coalition. This also makes illegal the arms trade to Saudi Arabia from the U.K., United States, and Sweden.

What Must Be Done

Resolution 2216 violates the UN Charter by putting the entire blame on one party to a domestic conflict. This violates the UN policy of reconciliation of parties and noninterference in domestic conflicts. Then it encourages the Saudi-led coalition to enforce the disarmament of the party blamed, the Houthis, with a war on Yemen.

But the implementation of Resolution 2216 also involves grave illegalities: The UN does not allow starvation or other war crimes in the implementation of its policies and resolutions.

To bring in food and end the war, it is most urgently necessary to compel a change in the implementation of Resolution 2216.

Pressure from both international NGOs and governments is absolutely necessary.

On December 6, 2016 Oxfam demanded the lifting of the import restrictions to Yemen for food, fuel, and medicine. Mark Goldring, Oxfam GB Chief Executive,

was quoted in a press release: "Yemen is being slowly starved to death. First there were restrictions on imports—including much need food. When this was partially eased the cranes in the ports were bombed, then the warehouses, then the roads and the bridges. This is not by accident—it is systematic. The country's economy, its institutions, its ability to feed and care for its people are all on the brink of collapse. There is still time to pull it back before we see chronic hunger becoming widespread starvation. The fighting needs to stop and the ports should be fully opened to vital supplies of food, fuel and medicine."

Earlier, on August 16, twelve international humanitarian NGOs had demanded that the restrictions on civilian air traffic to Yemen be lifted. The twelve were ACF International, ACTED, Care, Danish Refugee Council, Global Communities, Handicap International, International Rescue Committee, Intersos, Mercy Corps, Norwegian Refugee Council, Oxfam, and Save the Children.

It is urgent to address these illegalities now, to stop the genocide. It is especially urgent at this moment, because the Saudis have just decided to re-enforce their blockade of Houdeida, the only harbor that can reach the majority of the population in Yemen.

III. LaRouche's Musical Breakthrough of 1995

That Which Underlies Motivic Thorough-Composition

by Lyndon H. LaRouche, Jr.

Author's Introduction: Aug. 8, 1995—During several hours, on Sunday afternoon, July 30, five of us discussed the perspective on writing the crucial, thematic element of the Music Manual's Volume Two: Motivic Thorough-Composition: John and Renée Sigerson, Bruce Director, Dennis Speed, and I. This included an intense discussion of the philosophical basis which made Motivführung *a necessary scientific discovery, for Haydn, Mozart, Beethoven, et al.*

This included emphasis upon the pedagogical challenges posed by the need to precede the presentation of motivic thorough-composition, by proof of the necessity of its being discovered: just as the natural construction of the human speaking/singing apparatus required the development of a well-tempered C=256 scale as a precondition for perfected polyphonic composition. For absent friends and collaborators, who should have participated, from Eisenach, Wiesbaden, and also that metropolis known to all as Elsewhere, this aide-memoire is produced.

The proposition posed by Book II of **A Manual on Tuning and Registration,**[1] presents the editors of that book with the following pedagogical challenge.

Prompted by Josef Haydn's string quartet, Opus 33, No. 3, Wolfgang Mozart revolutionized musical composition, beginning the years 1782-86. This, Mozart accomplished by examining the discovery which Haydn expressed in the first movement of that quartet, in the light of the methods of polyphonic modality appearing, chiefly, in the work of J.S. Bach, notably the example of Bach's celebrated **A Musical Offering.** The result was Mozart's famous elaboration of an improved method of composition, sometimes identified as *Motivführung,* which we identify generically as "motivic thorough-composition."

Later, as exemplified by his late string quartets, Beethoven, during the last decade of his life, introduced a fundamental advance in Mozart's discovery, a richer modality in motivic thorough-composition. This method, its foundations so noted, dominated those great works of the Classical repertoire which were composed during the interval 1782-1897, from Mozart's discovery, to the death of Johannes Brahms.

The task of assembling Book II of that Music Manual obliges us to put these and closely related issues foremost, in the same sense that the historically determined discovery of the natural principles of well-tempered tuning, registration, and vibrato of the adult, *bel canto* singing voice, were put forward as the subsuming conception of Book I. That implicit obligation is described summarily, as follows.

From 1782 through the time of the deaths of Beethoven and Franz Schubert, saw the completed development of the crucial features of those forms of composition, and also of the performing instruments and their ensembles. Later, Brahms, most notably, enriched the development of those methods of motivic thorough-composition, but without altering the principles laid down by Beethoven. Although various developments of the construction and use of the instruments, both good and bad, were continued after 1828, today's most advanced principles of both Classical motivic thorough-composition, and the definition of the roles of the instruments and ensembles in performing such works, were fixed by the combined standards of Beethoven's **Missa Solemnis, Ninth Symphony,** and late string quartets. With such qualifications, it is accurate to say, that, by the time of Beethoven's death, the musical palette, and the contributing functions of its in-

---

1. See **A Manual on the Rudiments of Tuning and Registration,** Book I, John Sigerson and Kathy Wolfe, eds., (Washington, D.C.: Schiller Institute, 1992).

Lyndon LaRouche (left) and Norbert Brainin, the first violinist of the former Amadeus Quartet. In 1990, Brainin, in discussions with LaRouche, identified the revolutionary breakthroughs in Haydn's and Mozart's compositions in the 1782-86 period, as "Motivführung"— a discovery whose mastery LaRouche instantly recognized as the key to unleashing a renaissance in Classical musical composition.

struments and ensembles, were defined in approximately the same degree J.S. Bach's last years defined the principles of well-tempered polyphony.

The Manual is now proceeding toward completion of its original design, from the treatment of the singing voice, in Book I, into the treatment of the other instruments, in Book II. At this point, the governing principles of our effort are chiefly twofold. First, in both Books, the well-tempered tuning and registration of the human *bel canto* singing voice, is primary; the instruments and ensembles of the Classical palette remain, to this day, man-made extensions of the human individual's *bel canto* singing voice. Everything said in Book I, applies to the instrumental voices and ensembles of Book II. Second, the driving force in the reshaping of the requirements of the instruments and ensembles, from 1782 onward, is the changes in use of the ensemble, relative to the work of Carl Philip Emanuel Bach, for example, under the impact of the use of the new form of motivic thorough-composition wielded by such minds as Mozart, Haydn, and Beethoven. In short, to understand the instruments, one must situate the development of those instruments, and of their use, within that compositional setting which shaped their evolution.

This does not exclude consideration of relevant aspects of pre-1782, or post-1828 developments. Rather, the concentration upon 1782-1828 provides the historical benchmark of choice, from which to reference that which leads into 1782, and that which flows from it.

This evolutionary development of the instruments and ensembles could not be adequately represented without showing the new motivic method of composition, as the characteristic, determining feature of that process. Acknowledging that obligation, creates, in turn, an additional problem: a crucial problem of editorial, or, better said, pedagogical policy, a crucial issue of method.

In a precociously incautious impulse, one might presume that it were sufficient to present the principles of motivic thorough-composition, with suitable examples, as a matter of specialist education. That would be as if to say to the reader: "Learn the principles and techniques of motivic thorough-composition, and you will see how this new method of composition changed not only the method for composing Classical music, but the requirements of the instrumental performance." For the *Brotgelehrten* of musical academia, that would be the acme of professionalism.

For us, such preciosity, such pedantic narrowness, such a fallacy of composition would be *morally* repulsive! In Book I, we fulfilled a moral obligation, to demand nothing from blind faith: We supplied the reader a *transparent* view of the necessary origins and development of well-tempered *bel canto* tuning and registration. The same must be done, in Book II, for the principles of motivic thorough-composition.

In Book I, we demonstrated that the *bel canto* principles of well-tempered singing-voice tuning and registration were a necessary development within music (and that Helmholtz and Ellis, and their devotees, were no more than charlatans). The same is true for *Motivführung*, and must be shown, similarly.

The difference between the respective endeavors of Books I and II, so compared, is that the principle of *Mo-*

Wilhelm Furtwängler in Berlin, 1930. He chided certain conductors, to learn to perform "between the notes."

Société Wilhelm Furtwängler

tivführung goes directly to the most fundamental principles of the human mind. If that appears, at first encounter, as a frightening prospect, we might console ourselves in three ways. First, is it not fitting, that the second book of an educational series, should be more profound, and challenging conceptually, than the forerunner? Second, this writer and his relevant associates command readily identifiable, unquestionably unique, scientific competencies for addressing these underlying issues of composition. Third, we are at the point, that the mere process of continued ageing of the dwindling relative handful of musicians who know Classical principles, would relegate the literate reading of those musical scores to a lost art; this introductory task we must undertake, is a compelling one.

That noted, we now outline, step by step, the underlying principles of the human mind, upon which the necessity for motivic thorough-composition is premised.

The Curtain Rises

The art of musical performance is premised upon the creative powers of human memory. The experience of every notable musician, might readily affirm at least that much of the matter which is set before you here.

The matter goes, far beyond such acknowledgments, to an empyreal realm, far above anything of which all but a few greats among musicians, thus far, have shown themselves aware. When Wilhelm Furtwängler chided certain conductors, to learn to perform "between the notes," he demonstrated, that, even among leading conductors, there was an unmet need to master those most fundamental musical principles which are tucked away within the great art of memory, principles hidden by the speckled score, hidden "between the notes." Furtwängler's critics failed to comprehend, that he was pointing them toward functions residing within the domain of the power to remember. He was pointing them, not to a sensation, as a beastly melody might do, but rather to something exquisitely, beautifully human, an idea. In that instance, this signifies, as we do here: the essential quality of any musical idea.

Until one has uncovered, and developed those principles of musical memory, he or she might enjoy good musical composition and performance, but without understanding how to reproduce either at will, or why. Obviously, we could not be referring to so-called "rote memory." What kind of memory, then? To answer that last question, travel within the realm of memory itself, to recall some stunningly beautiful musical performance. Recall an outstanding experience from among those memories. Or, perhaps, the musician who might be serving as the student's teacher, would supply an appropriate demonstration of the principles we outline below.

Think back, in memory, to the moment the soloist appeared on stage. Block out from your recollection of that occasion, the sounds of applause, or kindred distractions; from the moment the soloist first appears before your eyes, hear nothing but the musical performance, until the last tone has vanished, into what is, for your memory of the event, a perfected auditory stillness. Perhaps, you have performed, either publicly, or alone with the music; if so, compare your recall of the soloist's performance of the first composition of that occasion, with memory of your own experience alone with the music. Make these recollections the subject-matter of your conscious deliberation. Concentrate on seeking out the function which memory performs in those events.

Then, add a slightly different recollection. Not of a soloist, but a duet. Let us term this, a recollection of a second type. Recall an evening of Schubert Lieder performed by a gifted singer and pianist, or a masterful performance of a Mozart, Beethoven, or Brahms violin sonata. As the reader will discover here, but a bit later, there is a compelling purpose in suggesting that you limit yourself, initially, to those three composers.

Next, recall a third type of musical event, a Mozart, Haydn, or Beethoven string quartet or quintet. At first, do not include Beethoven's late compositions. We might consider other composers, and other types of musical events; but, these three will be sufficient for the moment. As the first steps which we must walk in this direction, take these three types of musical events as a manifold. For the moment, register the fact that we are employing the term "manifold" in the sense common to both Bernhard Riemann's habilitation dissertation and the famous paradox of Plato's **Parmenides** dialogue. Adopt that musical manifold as the initial choice of subject-matter for our conscious attention; locate there, the functions of musical memory affecting the quality of the performance.

Later, we shall be prepared to move toward a higher objective: those principles of advanced motivic thorough-composition which are presented by Beethoven's late string quartets.

Now, let us merely describe the three, clearly distinguishable qualities of memory, which are guiding the musician performing on the stage of your memory. After those descriptions are supplied, turn to examine the concrete forms of the mental processes to which they correspond in the musician on stage.

Foremost, is the memory of the composition as an indivisible, continuing unit of conception, from the first to the last tone of its performance. To avoid a musical disaster on stage, this idea must remain constant, in the performer's mind, from a point prior to the performance of the first interval, until the perfected silence which follows the proper execution of the concluding tone. Second, there is a series of transitions, which define the evolutionary process of emergence of that indivisible conception, the which corresponds to the idea of the composition taken as a whole. Each of those transitions exists as an indivisible unit-idea; in the course of the performance, these intervals parade in their proper succession, as directed to do so by the controlling influence of the unit-idea of the composition as an entirety. Third, there is the idea of the process of development, linking each transition to its predecessor. Each moment of the development between transitions, is governed, twofoldly, by the idea of the transition, and under the governance of the unit-idea. If this rule is violated, musical coherence of the performance will not be achieved.

These three forms of mental processes are not merely descriptive, not merely pedagogical conveniences. Their definitions leap out at us from the performance, once we concentrate our attention upon the fact, that each of these three classes of ideas, which are controlling the performance, are recalled from memory, and are each products of memory. Once the answer is shown, we see, that, as in all truly rigorous scientific work: Up to that point of discovery, the solution to the riddle was being hidden from us by the obvious. Examine the function of these three kinds of ideas of memory.

In summary: What is the most crucial single fact which stands out for a modern Socrates, as we examine your recollection of the soloist's performance you have chosen, as we examine that from the vantage-point we have now described? The crucial fact is this. In order to conduct a coherent performance, which expresses the entire composition with singleness of effect, the soloist must have in view, from the beginning, the cumulative effect, the musical idea, to be reached with the final note.

Implicitly, what we have just said, obliges us to examine this matter of memory on a time-scale. We discover, immediately, that there is something essential in the influence of the musical idea upon the performance, the which can not be explained as an attributed epiphenomenon of the tone's sensation. There is a contradiction, a devastating paradox, which can be, and is heard as a musical idea, an idea which can not be attributed to the senses as such.

That devastating paradox is situated thus: See how the idea of the performance as an entirety, shapes the performance of the intervals addressed within each moment of the performance. We are confronted immediately with the existence of two musical ideas, both representing the composition taken as an entirety.

One of these two is efficiently superior to the other. The first of these two, is the performer's earlier grasp of the perfected idea of the composition as a finished whole; that is the idea which should never change in the musician's mind during the execution of the performance. This idea, the musician brings to the performance from an earlier, relatively perfected experience of the composition's completed performance.

The second idea, also pertaining to the composition as an entirety, is the notion of the incompleted idea of the same whole, in process of emergence, not yet *reperfected*: at each point mid-performance. The same principle governs not only the performance, and the practice leading to the performance of that composition; it is also the experience of the hearer.

The first must control the second. The tension between these two, axiomatically distinct qualities of idea of the composition as a whole, is readily recognized as the motivating "tension," that sense of "suspension," which supplies a quality of psychic intensity, which is to be perceived as the "energy" of the successful performance.

It is in this way, that each hearing affects one's conception of the perfected (completed) composition as an entirety. Each new hearing, or each new treatment of the performance of the work, in public or in private practice, affects the conception of the composition as a completed entirety. Each modification of the idea of the work as a perfected entirety (the first type of idea), affects the tension between that idea and the idea associated with the unfolding of the composition at each instant of mid-performance.

Thus, the paradox is situated. The unfolding of the second type of idea, the idea of the composition in the process of becoming, proceeds in a forward sense of time, from the first interval of the composition to the concluding tone. The idea of the composition as a completed entirety, the first type of idea, is represented as its impact of the completed performance upon the incompleted performance, upon the process of reproducing the performance yet to be completed. The first idea stands, thus, as representing a reversed ordering in time, in contrast to the naive sense-perception of the performance.

Contrast to this the viewpoint of the naive observer. He would tend to the proposition, that at any point in mid-performance, the idea of the composition in progress is based upon the "non-teleological," cumulative effect of what has been presented up to that relative point of time in the performance. In fact, at every point of a competent performance, it is the future (the idea of the work as a completed entirety), rather than the events of the relative past, which exerts the dominant influence on the manner in which each performed interval must be shaped.

That is the paradox, the crux of the matter: The idea is shaped in both forward and reverse directions. That topological anomaly is the most crucial single fact about the role of memory in controlling the artist's performance.

So, the simple act of perfecting a musical performance shifts the axiomatic definition of music, away from the empiricist's bad metaphyics, in which music is treated as an epiphenomenon of the auditory sense, into those deeper reaches of the human mind where all great art and science commonly reside. Here, within those deeper reaches, is the proper location to examine the true roots of music, in the most ancient forms of the singing of Classical poetry. Here, in seeing what music and poetry share in common with the Classical plastic art-forms and science in general, we may encounter the necessary and sufficient reason, that memory would ultimately produce a Classical *Motivführung*, as the appropriate method of composition.

Poetry, Drama, Painting, and Science

Compare this paradox with the same paradox as it presents itself in the performance of Classical poetry. For the simplest suitable example, let us employ a familiar case, once again for this occasion: Goethe's **Mailied.** Until the final couplet, it is a poem by a master craftsman, but otherwise trivial. It is the final couplet which is the poem; yet, all of the couplets preceding that are essential, to make possible the effect evoked by that final couplet. The artist, in rendering that poem, must anticipate the final couplet, in proceeding, from the first, into the final one. In viewing Raphael's "School of Athens," his "Transfiguration," or Leonardo da Vinci's "Virgin of the Rocks," one must recognize that, in each of the three cases, two views are presented in the painting. The painting, in each case, is neither of the two views, nor a simple addition of the two; the painting—its idea—is the result of the developmental process produced by considering the two primary views in any sequence.

In the classical tragedy of Friedrich Schiller, the same proposition applies, as Schiller himself describes it. The drama begins with a germ, which has all of the elements of the unfolding tragedy, as potential, within it. This process of unfolding proceeds to a moment of decision, which Schiller identifies as the *punctum saliens,* at which the future consequence of the hero's flaw of moral character is visible. Part of the function of the ensuing conclusion of the tragedy, is to affirm the nature of the flaw, by showing the doom which flows from it. The second principal function of the tragic outcome, is

'May Day Celebration'

by Johann Wolfgang Goethe

How grandly nature
Shines upon me!
How glistens the sun!
How laughs the mead!

From countless branches
The blossoms thrust,
A thousand voices
From underbrush,

And joy ecstatic
Fills everyone.
O sun! O earth!
O risk! O fun!

O love, oh, lovely,
So golden fair
Like morning cloudlets
On that hill there!

You prosper grandly
The dew-fresh fields
With breath of flowers;
The whole Earth yields!

O maiden, maiden,
How I love thee!
Your eye's a-sparkle—
How you love me!

Just as the lark loves
Singing and sky,
And morning-blooms thrive
On heav'n-mists high—

So do I love you,
with throbbing heart,
Who give me the youth,
Joy, courage, art

To fashion new songs,
New dances free.
Be *ever* happy,
As you love me!

—Translation by John Sigerson

In 1771, the brilliant, 22-year-old poet Johann Wolfgang Goethe composed the poem *Maifest* ("May Day Celebration"), which later came to be popularly known as *Mailied* or *Maigesang* ("May Song"), because of the title which Ludwig van Beethoven assigned to his musical composition of the poem.

Up to the final two lines, the poem presents a steamy picture of the exuberant youth, bursting with creative ideas, but still so immature as to believe that he requires doses of below-the-belt stimulation in order to continue to create. The implications of the ceremonial dance around the Maypole are, of course, obvious, as are the springtime blossoms, thrusting from their buds. The sentiment is further reinforced by the numerous exclamations of "O …" and "How …" (In the German original, the word for "how" is the much more explosive *wie,* pronounced "vee.")

Beyond these, shall we say, hormonal features, the lines leading up to the final couplet show the selfishness of one who is, in Shakespeare's words "in love with love." Unlike with mature love, he loves the maiden not for her own creatire potential, but merely for how she is useful as a goad to his own creativity.

The final couplet, however, lifts poem, reader, and audience out of this moist banality. The poet exhorts the maiden to be *eternally* happy, in the way she loves him. The only way that the maiden could be *eternally* happy in this way, is to love *that in the poet which is eternal,* i.e., his creative works. So, one is suddenly shifted out of immaturity, and into the adult realm of self-conscious love, in which the poet sees his immortality reflected through the eyes of the beloved.

Our English translation somewhat dulls the full impact of these final two lines, which in the German are: *Sei ewig glücklich, / Wie du mich liebst. Sei* (pronounced like "zigh" to rhyme with "high"), is the imperative tense of the the German verb for "to be," and has a similar, but even greater verbal impact than the earlier repetitions of the German exclamation *wie*. Then, *wie* comes at the beginning of the next, and final, line—but no longer as a mere exclamation, but as a means of clinching the paradox between the final couplet and all that precedes it.

The metaphor of the poem—the solution to the paradox—transforms all that has gone before. Again, the original German is more precise in its means to attain that end: The final line in the fifth strophe, "How you love me," is *Wie liebst du mich,* while the poem's concluding line, "As you love me," is accomplished by simply rearranging the word order, into *Wie du mich liebst*—something which no English translation could ever fully capture.—*John Sigerson*

(For additional discussion of "Mailied," see, "Some Simple Examples of Poetic Metaphor," by Kenneth Kronberg, in "Symposium: The Creative Principle in Art and Science," Fidelio, Vol. III, No. 4.)

to demonstrate that this was avoidable, but for the flaw. However, both of these features of the conclusion exist but to serve a higher-order end: These elements of the drama are designed to evoke joyous optimism in the audience, to demonstrate that we may become efficiently conscious of those flaws, which, uncorrected, would doom us. The idea of the whole which leaps from the tragic conclusion, thus, is the idea which shaped the author's composition of the drama, and must shape the conduct of the actors and director at each moment in mid-performance.

In Classical art-forms, as in science, the ideas of art or science are not the kinds of conceptions associated simply with the experience of the senses. In every case, whether Classical art-forms, or science, the quality of idea which typifies art or science, corresponds to a solution to a corresponding paradox of the senses. Respecting this underlying connection between artistic and scientific ideas, we must place the emphasis here on the notion of causality, as "necessary and sufficient reason" is understood by Gottfried Leibniz, or as Reason is identified to the same effect by Johannes Kepler.

The same notion of causality conveyed by Leibniz's "necessary and sufficient reason," is expressed in musical performance by the role of the paradox just outlined, above. *It is the governance of each moment of the mid-performance by the guiding role of the idea of the entire composition's perfected result, which is causality in the musical domain of Haydn, Mozart, Beethoven, Schubert, and Brahms.* This is the notion of causation (Reason) in Kepler's work. This is causality for the founder of modern science, Nicolaus of Cusa, and for Plato before them all. For exactly this reason, all great scientists prefer the music of Bach, Mozart, Haydn, Beethoven, Schubert, and Brahms: That faculty of the human mind which is indispensable to valid discoveries of principle in physical science, is identical with the mental faculty by which the greatest music is composed and performed. The method of Classical composition which we identify here as *Motivführung,* or motivic thorough-composition, is the mode of composition which provides the most appropriate model of mental state for the accomplished scientific discoverer.

That is the key to the necessity underlying the discovery and development of motivic thorough-composition.

This underlying identity of the principles of causality in scientific discovery, and also in coherent musical composition, is the key to showing the historical neces-

sity, that the method of motivic thorough-composition should emerge, like well-tempered, *bel canto* polyphony, as an asymptote of that essential aspect of universal history which is progress of forms in musical composition and performance. The essence of motivic thorough-composition, is not contained within the forms with which it is associated. The essence of motivic thorough-composition, is, rather, the necessity for its coming into existence: *the necessary and sufficient reason* for its coming into existence.

To understand music, we must understand the way in which its existence is subsumed by that universal principle of causation which Leibniz terms *necessary and sufficient reason.* Consider that principle of causation from its earliest documented appearence within human knowledge, within Plato's dialogues. Locate the connection of this principle to music, by considering several of the most crucial, most commonplace, but least known principles underlying the common use of spoken language.

It is important, to preface the point, respecting causality, to be developed next, by asserting unconditionally, that Plato's **Parmenides** dialogue must be read as the opening, thematic piece in a series of all Plato's later dialogues. It states, as a devastating ontological paradox, the proposition which those other dialogues address.

For the same reason just given above, respecting the performance of musical compositions, no one should waste his or her time mooting the silly scholars' squabbles respecting the relative, putative dates of writing of each among those dialogues. Ideas do not appear at the moment they are published; any person who has developed more than one valid idea in his or her life, knows, that ideas are written out for publication whenever the circumstances prompt this, not when those ideas are first conceived.

In any coherent mind, as Plato exemplifies this quality, ideas exist in the relative conceptual order of "necessary predecessor," "necessary successor." The order of ideas of a coherent thinker is the order in which they must have occurred, according to that principle of "necessary predecessor," "necessary successor." No serious thinker would argue, that the order in which topics are published is compelling evidence, in itself, of the order in which the corresponding conceptions appeared in the mind of an author.

If one knows the ideas characteristic of Plato's later works, one must reject the notion that the **Parmenides** is anything but the prologue for, the "necessary predecessor" of the others. If one differs with that, one has understood nothing essential in any among those dialogues. As in the case of any important musical composition of the manifold under consideration, the ordering of the subsumed elements implies the constant idea which governs the unfolding of that series of elements, from the beginning to the close. Indeed, that principle is precisely the subject of the **Parmenides**: the issue of the controversy between the principal characters, Socrates and Parmenides, of the drama. The point made here, is, thus, of a very special type: a self-reflexive, "isoperimetric-like" image of any conception which mirrors its own mirror-image without predefined limit.

The relevant essential issue of the **Parmenides** is the issue of causality. That issue is expressed thus.

Given, a Many (i.e., a "manifold" in the specific sense employed by Riemann's habilitation dissertation), can that Many be expressed as a single idea, a single stroke of conception? Can the Many transitions, and developments linking transitions, all be subsumed under the directing governance of an unchangeable idea of the composition as a whole? The underlying issue posed in that way: Can the diversity of the universe be subsumed under a single, unchanging idea? For example: "Could God exist?" For Plato, He is the Composer, a term which Plato employs in the sense of composer of music or poetry (which, for Plato, are the same thing).

In that dialogue, Parmenides fails repeatedly in his futile attempts to meet that challenge. He fails, as would the biologist, who, asked to define the principled distinction of living processes, responds by comparing the similarities and differences among species. In this dialogue, the key to Parmenides' self-humiliation is but briefly identified: Parmenides has left the principled role of *change* out of account. For Plato, this principle of change, is that of Heracleitus' frequently quoted aphorism: "Nothing is constant but change." Change, rather than things, is substance. On this point, return to the tension between the two, interacting ideas of a musical composition as an entirety.

For Plato, our idea of the perfected performance of the composition, the idea which does not change from the outset to conclusion of the performance, has the form of that which Plato identifies as the *Good*. The imperfected idea of the whole, existing at a moment in mid-performance, corresponds to what Plato identifies as the *Becoming*. This Becoming represents the ontological quality of that principle of change which subsumes a Many. The treatment of these matters of Good and Becoming, flows from the consideration of the ontological paradox posed by the **Parmenides,** through the elaboration provided in the dialogues which the **Parmenides** serves as a "necessary predecessor."

For comparison, consider the way in which the mathematician Georg Cantor applies Plato's respective notions of Good and Becoming to the domain of mathematics. For Cantor, Plato's Becoming is expressed in mathematics as the notion of the *Transfinite,* and Good as the mathematical *Absolute.* For Plato, Cusa, Kepler, and Leibniz, among others, the tension between the Good and the Becoming, is the form of causality in the universe as a whole: "necessary and sufficient reason." Think of these considerations from Plato in musical terms.

The practical significance, for us here, of the positioning of the **Parmenides** among Plato's later dialogues, is that the content of those later dialogues is the foundation upon which a rational comprehension of physical scientific knowledge, and comprehension of musical principles, depends. The relevant features of those dialogues are adduced only when one appreciates those features as responses to the ontological paradox posed by the **Parmenides.** For that reason, it is a commonplace fact, that anyone who attempts to compose a fraudulent representation of the dialogues of Plato, or of Plato's Socratic method as such, will usually suffer a compulsion to offer a fraudulent criticism of the **Parmenides.**

To meet our obligations here, the following summary of Plato's argument identifies the most relevant elements.

Follow Plato, as in his **Timaeus.** For him, God is the Composer of this universe. That composition corresponds to an idea, an idea which is unchanged from the beginning to the completion of the composition. That idea has the quality of Plato's Good, or what Cantor terms, alternately, as Absolute. In each instant of mid-performance, that composition is an unperfected Becoming; yet, the course taken by that Becoming, in each such instant, is shaped under the control of the Good. For Plato, or for the founder of modern science, Nicolaus of Cusa, for Kepler, and for Leibniz, that *musical* notion of the shaping of the Becoming by the Good is the meaning of Reason. The notion of natural law, whether in physical processes, or in society, is that same Reason.

Aristotle and his followers, including philosophical

materialists such as the modern empiricists, the Romantics, and the positivists, evade Plato's argument. Aristotle gave the name of the deceased "Plato" to a caricature, a *Golem* which he had fabricated for the purpose of intimidating the credulous. To wit: The Aristoteleans argue that Plato's "Good" is some final result, perhaps "at the end of time." Therewith, these ostensible critics raise a commotion over such misleading terminology as "Final Cause" and "teleology." On the premise of such straw-man arguments, they each plant their feet four-square in the quicksand of sense-certainty; they insist that the cause of today's object in motion can be nothing other than that which bumped that object yesterday. Out of that four-footed sense-certainty, they attribute any change which might not be explained in a percussive, or kindred fashion, to an epiphenomenon of Aristotle's **Metaphysics.**

The point so bumptiously illustrated, is that the end is not some mystical "Final Result"; like the changeless idea which shapes the enunciation of the composition at each instant of mid-performance, the end is now, and always. Aristotle, like his devotees, presents essentially no more than echoes of the same sophistry employed by Parmenides' Eleatics before him. The existence of the One which subsumes the Many, is rigorously implied by the principle of change which demonstrably orders the existence of the successive terms of the Many. From the action which shows the hand of the Good, the existence of the Good is known as One.

The musically relevant point to be made, coincides with my presentation of the crucial implications for economy, of Bernhard Riemann's **Hypothesen** dissertation. Riemann's discovery is so little known, and so much less understood, that no wasteful burden is placed upon the reader by recapitulating the immediately relevant essentials of that conception here. Riemann is rightly taken as restating a most relevant feature of Plato's notion in the terms of reference directly applicable to modern physical science.

Riemann's 'Becoming'

Put to one side, those warped mathematicians who speak of "the curvature of physical space-time." Riemann's often misrepresented discovery (as set forth first in his **Hypothesen** habilitation dissertation of June 1854) has the following principal import for the notion of causality in mathematical physics, and for the principle of motivic thorough-composition in music. The argument, in summary, proceeds as follows.

Today's generally accepted university-classroom mathematics, finds its origins in a creation of the naive imagination, in an image of space-time like that offered by a traditional classroom reading of Greek geometry. In that naive fantasy, space is defined axiomatically in terms of three primary senses of direction, which are assumed to be extensible, both without limit, and with perfect continuity: backward-forward, up-down, and side-to-side. To time is attributed a single sense of direction: backward-forward. The principal postulates of that notion of quadruply-extended space-time, are the arbitrary assumption that points exist as infinitely small regions of space, whose magnitude is absolute zero, and that a "straight line" is the shortest distance between two points in space. These postulates are required by the axioms of the trebly-extended space manifold.

Neither sense-certainty, nor such a mathematics makes any provision for the existence of cause within our universe.

The attempt to develop a mathematical physics consistent with that naive sort of quadruply-extended space-time manifold, consists of mapping the location of the points within an object such that those correspond to points in naively defined space. Change of that mapping, with respect to time, is assumed to represent a linear form of motion. Forms of change other than simple displacement in space-time, are defined naively in terms of the simple idea of motion. No provision for cause is supplied.

That species of naive mathematical physics comes into crisis when experimental evidence presents forms of motion, and related change, which can not be accounted for in terms of the axiomatic features of naive space-time. This was already noted by leading figures of Plato's Academy of Athens, and their followers, such as Aristarchus, Archimedes, and Eratosthenes. For example, simple astronomy showed that measurements on the surface of the earth required a spherical geometry, rather than a plane geometry. Kepler's discovery of a principle of universal gravitation from his work on the planetary orbits, is an example of this. Most significant is the impact of Ole R@tomer's 1677 astrophysical measurement of the "speed of light" at about 3×10^8 meters per second, which prompted Christiaan Huyghens to define principles of reflection and refraction, which, in turn, led Jean Bernoulli and Gottfried Leibniz to show that the "algebraic" mathematical physics of Galileo, Descartes, and Newton was incompetent for the domain of physical phenomena, and that a "non-algebraic" mathematics of the transcendental domain, was required, instead.

Each discovery of a physical consideration which causes motion to proceed along pathways contrary to the doctrine of existing mathematical physics, has an effect more or less similar to what Bernoulli showed for the generalized refraction of light. Each of these added considerations assumes the form of extension, in the sense that our naive ideas of space and time are premised upon a general notion of extension. This accumulation of extensions, beginning with notions such as "mass" and of "refraction of a constant rate of retarded propagation of light," represents such a notion of extension. The accumulation of such notions of extension prompts us to describe "physical space-time" by such terms as an "extended manifold of *n* dimensions."

All of these *n*-fold considerations correlate with our ideas of *measurement*, a measurement of action, of "change." Relative to our naive image of quadruply-extended space-time, these measurements which deviate from linear space-time notions of movement or related change, suggest "curvature": curvature of the relevant motion, or, more generally, relevant change.

It has been generally overlooked by commentators, that Riemann's argument takes us directly into the subjective domain. There should have been no doubt of this among Twentieth-Century scholars, who had the crucially relevant, posthumously published works before them: the **Metaphysik und Psychologie** implicitly referenced, in mention of Herbart together with Gauss, in the **Hypothesen.** Simply, the development of the idea of the *n*-fold physical space-time manifold reflects a series of discoveries of physical principle: It is the word "discovery" which would persuade any alert scientist, that physics has proven itself to be a branch of rational psychology, a topic, like music, rooted in the subjective domain. This is the crucial feature of Riemann's discovery.

That crucial feature centers around the following issue. Like a modern positivist's perversion of a theory of musical counterpoint, all formal (i.e., deductive) mathematics has the form of a deductive theorem-lattice. That is to say, a set of propositions which have been elevated to the dignity of theorems, on the presumption that it has been demonstrated that each and all are not-inconsistent with an underlying set of interdependent axiomatic assumptions. A deductive form of mathematics for a quadruply-extended space-time, is an example of such a theorem-lattice; any formal math-

ematical representation of an *n*-fold physical space-time manifold, is an example of this.

Any change within the set of interdependent axioms of such a theorem-lattice, produces a new theorem-lattice which is formally and pervasively inconsistent with the lattice premised upon the unchanged set. In the language of both Plato and Riemann, any such set of interdependent axioms is termed an *hypothesis*; any change in the set, represents a new *hypothesis*.

It is to be noted, respecting any reading of Riemann's **Hypothesen** paper, or later papers on mathematical-physics topics, that this significance of the term "hypothesis/hypotheses" is the permeating theme of all Riemannian mathematical physics. Notably, it is upon this basis that Riemann exposed Isaac Newton as a bungling empiricist, a scientific illiterate (see "Why Most Nobel Prize Economists Are Quacks," **EIR,** July 28, 1995, p. 31, note 30).

Thus, each of the validated discoveries of principle which alter the preferred choice of *n*-fold physical space-time manifold, represents a change of theorem-lattice, a change in the set of interconnected axiomatic assumptions underlying mathematical physics. This change is predominantly a change in the ontological axiomatics, rather than the space-time form as such. The appropriateness of the new mathematics over the old is shown in the domain of measurement of motion, or of analogous action. There will be a change in the characteristic feature of measurement of such motion or other action. To this end, it is desirable, but not imperative that the correct measure be made; it is sufficient, at the outset, that it be shown that a certain quality of change in measurement is required.

Although the measurement itself lies ostensibly within the domain of what pedants reference as "scientific objectivity," the act of discovery which produces the appropriate new mathematics does not. Our attention should then be turned to the fact, that all valid science (and art, too) is the product of a faculty of discovery of this sort. There is an adducible principle presented to us by the evidence of the relatively valid discoveries of principle of all human knowledge to date: the unique faculty, by means of which valid, axiomatic-revolutionary discoveries of principle are made. This faculty we name "creative reason," the faculty by which man and woman were known to the Moses of **Genesis** 1:26-30, to be made in the image of God the Creator.

This faculty of creative discovery, is the sole means by which mankind's power over nature has been increased from the ape-like potentials of several millions living individuals, to those potential relative population-densities, and associated improvements in demographic characteristics, which had become the benchmarks of human progress into the middle 1960s. This principle of creative discovery, which a child experiences each time he or she replicates the original act of discovery of some valid, axiomatic-revolutionary principle, is the proximate cause of the increase of mankind's power over nature per capita: It is the psychological cause of a physical effect. How do we represent that causation, mathematically?

Therewith comes the fun, the topic which is crucial for understanding motivic thorough-composition.

The inconsistency bridged by the transition from one theorem-lattice to another, has the mathematical, and mathematical-physical (i.e., ontological) quality of what is termed variously a (formally absolute) mathematical discontinuity, or a singularity. This might be depicted graphically by a point which is of unlimited smallness, but never mathematical zero, or a line whose thickness is, similarly, of unlimited, never-zero smallness. The increasing accumulation of valid axiomatic-revolutionary discoveries of principle, over the course of human existence to date, thus represents an accumulation of such discontinuities, an accumulation expressed as implicitly denumerable; thus, the transmission of that culture to a person today, awards that person a quality of knowledge which might be expressed in terms of *density of discontinuities per interval of action: action of thought.* In other words: describable as an *n*-fold physical space-time manifold. This form of manifold, associated with functions of increasing density of such discontinuities, is characteristic of *not-entropic* processes, such as living processes generally, the human cognitive functions, and the action which typifies successful societies.

Any musical composition which satisfies the requirements of motivic thorough-composition, has the same quality as creative scientific generation of a valid, new theorem-lattice. It is that quality of distinction, which defines the musical composition as a whole, as a unit musical idea unique to that composition. The kinds

Any musical composition which satisfies the requirements of motivic thorough-composition, has the same quality as creative scientific generation of a valid, new theorem-lattice. It is that quality of distinction, which defines the musical composition as a whole, as a unit musical idea unique to that composition.

of modal transitions which Wolfgang Mozart defined in practice, by his 1782-86, and subsequent development of a Bach-pivotted method of motivic thorough-composition, are exemplary of this. Beethoven's revolution within Mozart's own motivic method, a revolution exemplified by the late quartets, is also exemplary of this. It is the modal feature which Mozart understood in the Bach **Musical Offering,** and the extension of that same modal principle by Beethoven, by a topological revolution in modalities, which exemplifies composition effected by a pure act of coherent creativity: the generation of a relatively absolute musical idea by means of a succession of revolutions in treatment of a pair of root-intervals, these representing, like the Bach/Mozart C-minor/C-major modality, a single modal germ.

Shifting focus back to Riemann for a moment: Apply Riemann's notion of hypothesis to the axiomatic-revolutionary progress of mathematical physics, to date. Let us, for purposes of first-approximation, apply that idea of the progress of physics in general, to the examination of this ongoing composition taken in mid-performance. We have an "objective" measurement, which shows us that this is progress: increase of potential relative population-density, a characteristic measurement of action of a society practicing a certain development of scientific knowledge. We should know, if we render ourselves conscious of the experience of replicating the act of discovery of valid axiomatic-revolutionary principles, the method of action—the notion of modality—by means of which the progress is generated. We are then prepared to treat the execution of scientific progress as an accomplished performer renders a great musical composition. We have then joined Plato and Kepler in knowing the universe as a composition. We have then joined Leibniz in comprehending the principle of necessary and sufficient reason. We have then addressed the significance of Riemann's discovery. We have then uncovered the importance of Mozart's and Beethoven's successive revolutions in the application of the principle of motivic thorough-composition.

Now, turn to the common root of music and mathematics, the *bel canto* vocalization of the spoken utterance.

Derrida's Cacophony

The communication of ideas within society is accomplished chiefly by aid of that spoken utterance, called speech, whose pale shadow is the written word. The idea communicated is contained within neither of the two verbal media, although properly sung oral utterance is much closer to reality than the **New York Times' Style Book,** or the presently popular, Derridaesque lunacies of the Modern Language Association (MLA)'s politically-correct "de-phonization" of the written language.

Oral utterance is vocalization, as the natural *bel canto* potentialities of the human speaking apparatus require. Oral utterance demands singing-voice registration as an essential component of written utterance. The literate form of spoken word, such as William Shakespeare's stage, for English, is a vastly more powerful medium than the written word, except to the degree that the reader, and also the writer, share the understanding that the written utterance is to be reconstructed, phonically, as it had been spoken, in a *bel canto* singing manner, with register shifts, as by a classically-trained actor of the Classical Shakespeare or Schiller theater. Competent punctuation, in opposition to the MLA and **New York Times' Style Book,** is applied to the purpose of prompting the reader to reconstruct the Classical—e.g., Shakespearean—form of oral utterance intended by the written passage. Great poetry, Classical tragedy, and the apotheosis of Classical poetry, as song composed in a mode of motivic thorough-composition, are the richest media for transmission of ideas in speech.

In oral, or written utterance, as in the great Wilhelm Furtwängler's musical performances, ideas sing between the words, as the musical idea sings between the notes of the score. Speaking broadly, the key to comprehending these distinctions, is *irony*; as Riemann's work illustrates the related case for mathematical physics, the idea-content of speech lies outside the narrow band-pass of either oral or written dictionaries and grammar, in the higher domain of *metaphor*. Symbolism, by contrast, is for the *Brotgelehrten,* the sexually hyper-active, the oafs, or to use a gentler term of reproof among professional musicians, *Romantics.* As in discovery of principle in science, ideas come into existence as formal discontinuities, as singularities.

Our palette presents us, thus, three distinct notions of spoken communication: first, the idea itself, which can not be contained within the band-pass of speech as such; second, the literate form of utterance, the highest form of communication; and, third, the written shadow of spoken utterance, which is literate only to the degree that the composer (author) and re-composer (reader) understand that the written text is supplied to the purpose of prompting the hearing of the implied, literate spoken utterance in the mind of the reader.

For example. A literate written text is that which, among other qualifications, is written and punctuated from a literate, e.g., a phonic, standpoint: to reflect voice-register shifts, to set off clauses and phrases serving as subjects, predicates, or appositives, and kindred speaking-voice requirements. An illiterate spoken text, is one which attempts to intone a written text in a sing-song, or any other among those otherwise stylized manners designed for oral rendering of written text, as typically acquired in classrooms or analogous settings.

Notably, the worst performances among musicians who have acquired physical and related qualities of technical proficiency, are derived most visibly—and painfully—from a carrying over, into reading of the musical score, of the tendency to read the written text of prose or poetry as if there existed a written language which had its own primary existence, rather than existing as a mere shadow of sung prosody. Long before there was the cacophonous doctrinal babbling of Jacques Derrida, there was already the well-established, psychosexually impotent belief in the original existence of text (as of score).

Within the domain of the professional musician, this fanatical perversion appears commonly as the dogma of "instrumental music." The customary root-doctrine on this point, is that of the Nazi-like cult of Dionysos and Richard Wagner, that music derives from dance, rather than the vocalization of poetry. These are the Dr. Sigmoid Frauds of the musical slums, existentialist followers of positivists such as Ernst Mach, doctrinaires of the ilk who attribute all aesthetical values to not only sensual effects as such, but, preferably, sexually-orgiastic ones.

The effort to promote a cult of "instrumental music," denying the ancestry of all music in the polyphonic vocalization of poetry, is the work of the existentialist "Derridas" of the musical salon and conservatory, and, of the like of the Austro-Hungarian *Geheimpolizei,* who administered the musical policy of the empire under such notorious "doges" of the *Fürstentum* as chancellors Wenzel von Kaunitz and Clement Prince Metternich. Similarly, in Metternich's circles in Prussia, the relevant administrators were the neo-Kantian Romantics G.W.F. Hegel and, more emphatically, the forerunner of the Hitler regime's philosophy of law, Friedrich Savigny.

Underlying this more immediately obvious parallel between the doctrines of text in literature, and of "instrumental music," there is a deep-going, causal connection.

Once those misleading presumptions of the written text have been placed to one side, thus, we may focus upon those crucial features of the relationship, between literate forms of oral utterance and music, which bear upon the origins of motivic thorough-composition.

Neither speech nor the literal aspects of a musical score, can convey ideas within that medium as such. As Classical poetry underscores the relevant aspect of spoken, and sung language, it is the metaphors which are the sole "repository," so to speak, of the actual ideas. This role of metaphor is the feature of poetry which the popularized doctrines of symbolic interpretation are supplied to conceal and deny.

The use of irony to achieve metaphor, is the most crucial feature of human speech, and of music, the aspect of communication which enables one mind to provoke the synthesis of an idea within the mind of another individual. All important ideas are of this form; they express the same problem, and solution, posed by the fact that an entire new theorem-lattice is separated from the predecessor which it replaces, by a single singularity (e.g., mathematical discontinuity). It is by breaking the bounds of literal reading of the existing usage of language, that metaphor enables us to enter a domain of relative higher *cardinality,* as from a manifold of n degrees of extension, to one of $n+1$ degrees. The precondition for this, is that the ironies associated with the metaphor are real, that they correspond to identifying a fallacy of principled assumption in the previously accepted use of that language.

Hence, the intrinsically pseudo-scientific character of so-called "infomation theory." Since the change introduced by the use of the metaphor defines implicitly an entirely new theorem-lattice, of higher cardinality, the quantifiable effect of the relevant communication is, axiomatically, vastly greater than the adducible absolute statistical potential of the medium employed.

The metaphor employed to this effect, can not be located within the channel of communication between

> **The use of irony to achieve metaphor, is the most crucial feature of human speech, and of music, the aspect of communication which enables one mind to provoke the synthesis of an idea within the mind of another individual.**

the speaker and the hearer. The channel reveals only the ironies with which both the speaker and the hearer associate the metaphor. The metaphor itself exists only in the minds of each of the persons, not within the medium of communication. It is upon this aspect of the matter that we must presently focus most intently.

For most readers, the principal source of the difficulty which the professionals experience with our line of argument, is the combined impact of two facts. First, all but a vanishing handful among them are either totally, or virtually bereft of consciousness of a Classical humanist method of education; the defects in their education have denied them the references which would make the notion of creative discovery readily accessible to one educated by that Classical method. Second, during the recent centuries, especially in the aftermath of British triumphs in wars, the empiricist method has also triumphed politically among not only the vanquished European nations—first France, and later Germany. After the premier opponent of British imperialism, the U.S.A., succumbed to a "special relationship" with Presidents Theodore Roosevelt's, Woodrow Wilson's, Coolidge's, Harriman's, and Bush's beloved Britain, the Svengalis of empiricist dogma have gradually subdued the Trilbys of the dominant educational and cultural institutions of the planet, and also the popular culture of western Europe and the Americas.

That source of difficulty need be identified and stressed, that the crucial point be made comprehensible. It must be stressed, that in a Classical humanist mode of education, as typified by the Wilhelm von Humboldt gymnasium program for Germany, the emphasis is upon the student's reliving the original act of discovery of the important discoveries of principle, in every leading department of knowledge, throughout history to date. In this way, instead of merely learning the answer, the student comes to know the answer. More significant, the student who benefits from such Classical rigor in education, is made conscious of his or her own creative-mental processes, by means of which the original discovery is replicated within the student's own mental processes. The result is to be compared with the musical case under consideration here.

In each case the student replicates the mental act of

discovery of an axiomatic-revolutionary quality of solution-principle, the student is doing much more than learning the textbook answer for the relevant examination question. By reliving the act of axiomatic-revolutionary discovery, with the student's own sovereign creative-mental powers, the student arrives at a relatively absolute idea, of the form of Plato's Good. This idea thereafter governs the student's re-replication of the act of discovery, as the idea of a completed musical composition acts to control the re-replication of the process leading toward a repetition of that completion. It is the tension, between that relatively Absolute idea, and the relative Becoming, the process of completing the discovery, which is the active expression of knowledge in that case.

This process can occur only within the creative-mental processes of the individual person; it can not be supplied in an articulate form in a medium of communication among persons. The communication-process's function, is not to communicate the idea of the discovery, but merely to prompt the mind of the hearer, to replicate the creation of that discovery.

In the case, that the speaker succeeds in prompting that replication in the mind of the hearer, we may speak of the speaker's expressed *insight* into the mental processes of the hearer. In that case, the speaker has employed his (or her) own mind, to construct, as a kind of "sub-set" of his own mind, a kind of analog of the hearer's mind. His object, is to select a pattern of "signals," which, expressed through a medium of communication, will tend to prompt the hearer's mind to engage in the desired process of creative replication. In sum: Classical-humanist pedagogy, as distinct from the deplorable, empiricist kind. The gifted composer, such as a Bach, Haydn, Mozart, Beethoven, Brahms, employs the same principles of Classical-humanist pedagogy to compose, and to teach their students, just as Wilhelm Furtwängler devised his tricks for evoking the necessary, but unsayable musical result from his orchestras.

Real ideas do not exist within the "band-pass" of any medium of communication, of spoken or written language, or formal mathematics, included. Nor, could they ever be replicated by a digital computer. They exist only within the human mind. The function of communication, is to enable one individual mind to prompt a replication of the creative-thinking process in other human minds, much as Furtwängler shaped the musical insights of the musicians within his orchestras.

It is a matter of measurement. Living processes, discovery of valid scientific principles, the use of those creative processes to generate or to replicate artistic ideas, and scientific and technological economic progress, are each and all "not-entropic" processes. That is to say, that the characteristic measurement of the relevant, distinguishing form of action is "not-entropic." This can not be measured by any possible linear, or merely "non-linear" standard of measurement. Only the sovereign creative-mental processes wholly internal to the individual human mind, can generate, or willfully replicate a "not-entropic" conception.

Within the relatively entropic domain of formal mathematics, written language, grammatical utterance, or musical score, there is no place for creative ideas to dwell, except as discontinuities. These discontinuities dwell among, but not within the words, the mathematical formulations, the notes of the musical score. They are expressed by aid of the ironies whose manifest effect is to generate discontinuities. The ideas to which those discontinuities correspond, as do footprints to the person who walked that path, exist for language, for mathematics, and for music, only in that empyreal subjunctive where all true metaphors reside. For music, they are to be heard by the individual's inner ear of insight, between the notes.

Thus, in literate forms of language, we have three objects to consider: the spoken utterance, the written shadow of the spoken utterance, and the object to which the utterance refers, but only the inner mind of the utterer can know. In all cases of those concepts which deserve the reputation of knowledge, the essential concept is relatively Absolute, in the sense of the form of Plato's Good. The essential concept controls a second, subsumed version of the same concept, in the form of Becoming, in the process of emergence. Every other idea is subsumed by the electrifying tension of the interaction between these two.

Thus: 'Motivführung'

From the vantage-point of memory, the desired general goal in the development of methods of musical composition, is an increase in coherence: that each step in mid-performance, from the first to the last, brings the process of becoming into coherence with the indivisible idea of the composition as a whole. This must be achieved with the relatively greatest power, or apparent "energy" of the performance, which can be achieved only by increasing the density of discontinuities per interval of action. In other words, the intensity of the development. As the third movement of Beethoven's Opus 132 quartet, the *Heiliger Dankgesang,* epitomizes this, the most challenging development must be achieved with the most concerted expression of *agapic* beauty.

A not uncommon misunderstanding of Beethoven's later compositions, notably the late string quartets, supplies negative illustration of this point. The dupe of the modern musicologists' Hegelianizing, is soaked in a mystical delusion which might appear to have been first induced in the following manner.

According to imputable legend, the deed was done by the plainclothes *Poltergeister* of the Austro-Hungarian secret police, who, at the moment, lurked in the nooks and crannies of the 1814-15 Vienna Congress. One moonless night, while the delegates to the Congress were distracted by some drunken celebration, out from their lurking-places, slipped the evil earth-spirits of the mystical Central-European underworld. They moved by shadow, to shadow, into the musical neighborhoods; there, from the infants in their cradles, they ripped out the capacity to compose and hear music in a Classical mode (which, incidentally, had been performed at Johann Sebastian Bach's A=430 cycles). One could hear the monsters' fiendish giggling (*sotto voce*, of course), as, into the minds of the ravished infants, they inserted the changeling souls: the dispositions to compose, perform, and hear in the politically correct, Romantic manner (tuned to mad Czar Alexander I's A=440 cycles). All of this substitution was decreed, and duly notarized, over the great seal of Chancellor Metternich. In the morning, the blurred senses of the late-awakening households' members noted little change, except, perhaps, that the diapers were somewhat dirtier than usual.

Thus, according to the fantasy told by balding musicologists to the gaping credulous, 1815 marks the point in time, at which the Classical impulse within composers, performers, and audiences vanished, and the Romantic impulse pervaded the universe, instead. A fairytale? Perhaps; but, what the modern musicologists describe as the result, if true, could not have occurred in a way much different than the account we have just reported here.

This, sadly, is not the end of the tale. Near the turn of the century, the prank was repeated, once again in Vienna. The same imps, from 1815, now replaced their Romantic changelings with Modernist ones. This time, the morning diapers were terrible.

One might wonder, if news of the latter event trickled down to G.W.F. Hegel, wherever he resides, below. If so, Hegel and his old crony, Friedrich Savigny, shared a fiendish smile. Many musicologists, to the present day, appear to think so.

The principal evidence supporting this snippet of feudal folklore, is that modernized audiences pretend, at least, to enjoy the mauling of not only post-1815 Classical compositions, but also Mozart, as parodies of the style, perhaps, of Hector Berlioz. Sometimes, the works of Beethoven are appreciated almost as if they were smudges composed by Stockhausen; certainly, the late string quartets have been prey to such mistreatment more than once. It is a matter of dogma for some, that they must impose the raucous sound of their pedantic conceits upon Beethoven's intent; the supernal beauty of the *Heiliger Dankgesang* does not penetrate the thick brain-callous of their indoctrination.

If the unchanging idea of the perfected composition, must govern the performance in progress, from beginning to end, can not the idea of this relationship inspire the composer to improve the method of composition accordingly? Should the idea of the composition as a perfected whole, not guide the composer in his building the composition, step by step? Thus, to achieve a less imperfect coherence, in the process of composition itself, must we not desire, that the idea of the perfected composition should be, like a Schiller tragedy, an implication of some simple germ, from which the composition as a whole unfolds?

Can not the relationship, between the intended Absolute idea of the composition, and that germ, not be the generating principle under whose governance ("tension," "energy") the composition itself unfolds? As soon as we progressed, from formalist's modulation among keys, into the integration of a complex of keys into a single mode (as the Bach C-major/C-minor mode illustrated the point for the Wolfgang Mozart provoked by Haydn's new quartets), the required new idea of composition was implicitly identified. Once Mozart's notion of motivic modalities were drawn beyond its initial limits, by a genius such as the matured Beethoven, music may expand the range of modalities greatly, as he, at the outset, doubled the number of apparent keys we must recognize as awaiting us within a *bel canto* well-tempered system.

That revolution within the bounds of the Classical methods of well-tempered polyphony is not an arbitrary, if clever innovation, which one might choose to adopt or ignore. It is the unevadable solution to a profound scientific, and moral problem. Once we had adduced that Platonic function of memory, which renders Classical composition a way of representing the lawful ordering of the universe (this, according to what Leibniz recognizes as necessary and sufficient reason), we could not have been satisfied, until we had freed future musical composition from the pretty bric-a-brac extraneous to that principle. The discovery of motivic thorough-composition, satisfies that requirement.

The added obligation, which we must impose upon all composition in this expanded, nobler modality, is that it must never cease to be heard in the mind, and so displayed, as a domain of empyreal beauty.

Finally, before leaving this stage, to make way for the ensuing presentation of *Motivführung* as such, we must now turn to our culminating point. We must show why we selected the manifold we identified at the outset of this exposition. In light of what we have reviewed thus far, consider the species of apparent difficulties presented to the musical performers as we shift from the soloist, to the duet, and then to the quartet or quintet. Define, as a single conception, the common solution-principle for each and all among those cases.

The key to that manifold, is the sovereign creative powers of the individual mind. For reasons identified earlier here, the performance of great music, must employ the powers of insight, by both the composer and performer, to provoke the generation of the idea from, separately, and more or less simultaneously within each mind of the audience. So, the musicians on stage must interact with one another, to produce the same result as a combined effect of their performance.

So, the essential idea of musical performance, begins with the singer, singing his own composition, as accompanied, like Plato or Leonardo da Vinci, by his own lyre, or a Wolfgang Mozart or Beethoven performing one of his own previously composed solo works. A musician's performance of another's composition, introduces a new dimension: The performer must recreate the mind of the composer within his own, and let the composer's intent provide the insight into the mind of the audience. In a duet, performing the work of a great, but deceased composer, the performers add a new dimension to the challenge. With the Classical quartet or quintet, the challenge met in the duet, is drawn to the limit.

With the orchestra, the underlying principle is the same, but the problem of execution is somewhat different. In the transition from thorough-composed works for duets, trios, quartets, and quintets, to the orchestra, or large chorus, a new manifold is introduced. The emergence of the specific role of the musical director parallels the shift from the individual performer, of the first performing manifold, from the performer-voice, to the performer's participation in the voice of a part. In place of the individual musician performing a voice, several or more musicians participate in reproducing a part-voice; the function of their sovereign individuality, as performer, is shifted in that manner and qualitative degree. Otherwise, the deeper principle, common to both performing manifolds, remains the same. With that qualification, our attention can be focussed upon the smaller scale of performing manifold.

The key to the role of the individual performer, in the smaller manifold, is already signalled in the score, in a close reading of the composer's treatment of polyphony. This serves, later, as also the key to the transition from the smaller to larger musical-performance manifold. The polyphony is already a manifold of human singing voices. This polyphony is the drama which the musician, or ensemble, must perform; that provides the key to the composer's insight into the minds of that audience to which the performers must deliver the intended result, the intended musical idea.

These matters are not to be seen as idiosyncrasies of the musical domain. They are those characteristics of well-tempered musical composition and performance which render music in general an indispensable spiritual nourishment of the agapic creative powers of reason, as creative work may occur in any honorable profession. These characteristics, perfected in execution in the degree motivic thorough-composition represents, are identical to the creative powers of valid, fundamental scientific discovery. These matters of music are not optional, not matters of taste, but indispensable habits for the maintenance and progress of civilized existence.

Classical Music, like the Negro Spiritual addressed by Brahms's Antonin Dvořák, is the apotheosis of that empyreal beauty which is known in science, as the submission of the human creative will to a principle, a principle which Gottfried Leibniz identified as *necessary and sufficient reason.* Like the development of J.S. Bach's well-tempered mode of natural *bel canto* polyphony, motivic thorough-composition, otherwise named *Motivführung,* is a natural and necessary realization of that principle.

That, my friends, is a principle to be committed to memory.